Street by Street

KINGالسال UPON HULL

BARTON-UPON-HUMBER, BEVERLEY

Anlaby, Barrow upon Humber, Bilton, Bransholme, Brough, Cottingham, Hedon, Hessle, North Ferriby, Preston, Skidby, South Cave, Sproatley, Swanland

3rd edition June 2008
© Automobile Association Developments Limited 2008

Original edition printed January 2003

 Enabled by | Ordnance Survey® This product includes map data licensed from Ordnance Survey® with the permission of the Controller of Her Majesty's Stationery Office. © Crown copyright 2008. All rights reserved. Licence number 100021153.

The copyright in all PAF is owned by Royal Mail Group plc.

Published by AA Publishing (a trading name of Automobile Association Developments Limited, whose registered office is Fanum House, Basing View, Basingstoke, Hampshire RG21 4EA. Registered number 18/8835).

Produced by the Mapping Services Department of The Automobile Association. (A03712)

A CIP Catalogue record for this book is available from the British Library.

Printed by Oriental Press in Dubai

The contents of this atlas are believed to be correct at the time of the latest revision. However, the publishers cannot be held responsible or liable for any loss or damage occasioned to any person acting or refraining from action as a result of any use or reliance on any material in this atlas, nor for any errors, omissions or changes in such material. This does not affect your statutory rights. The publishers would welcome information to correct any errors or omissions and to keep this atlas up to date. Please write to Publishing, The Automobile Association, Fanum House (FH12), Basing View, Basingstoke, Hampshire, RG21 4EA. E-mail: streetbystreet@theaa.com

Ref: ML152y

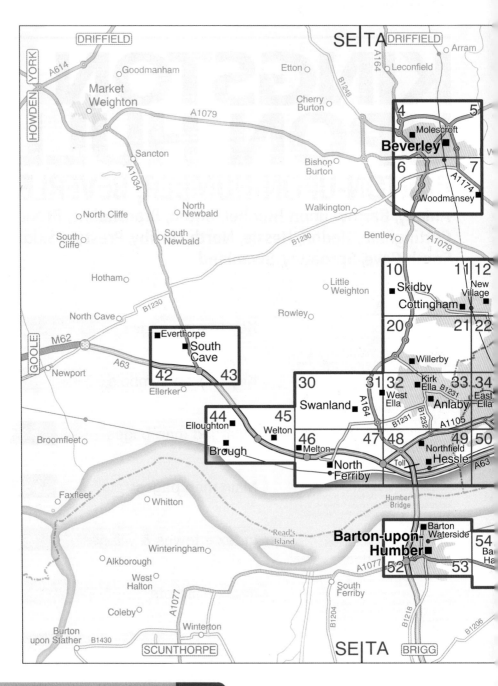

Scale of enlarged map pages **1:10,000** 6.3 inches to 1 mile

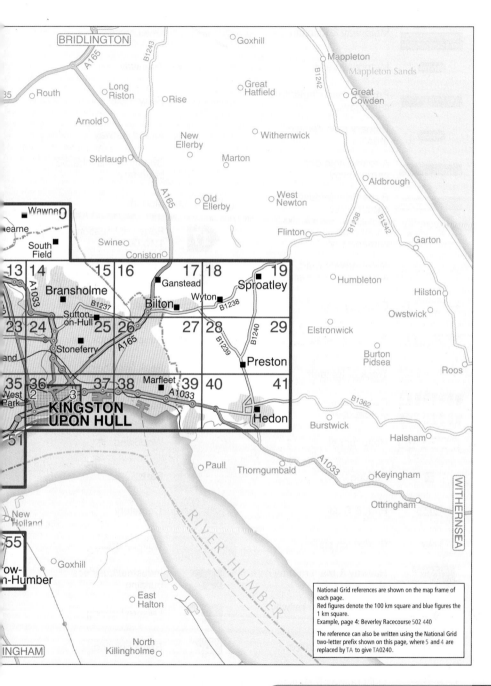

BRIDLINGTON

Goxhill

Mappleton

Mappleton Sands

35

Routh

Long Riston

Rise

Great Hatfield

Great Cowden

Arnold

New Ellerby

Withernwick

Skirlaugh

Marton

Aldbrough

Wawne

Old Ellerby

West Newton

Garton

earne

South Field

Swine

Flinton

Coniston

Humbleton

Hilston

13	14	15	16	17	18	19

Bransholme

Ganstead

Sproatley

Owstwick

Bilton

Wyton

Sutton-on-Hull

23	24	25	26	27	28	29

Stoneferry

Elstronwick

Burton Pidsea

and

Preston

Roos

35	36	37	38	39	40	41

West Park

Marfleet

KINGSTON UPON HULL

Hedon

Burstwick

Halsham

51

New Holland

Paull

Thorngumbald

Keyingham

Ottringham

WITHERNSEA

55

Goxhill

ow-n-Humber

East Halton

RIVER HUMBER

INGHAM

North Killingholme

National Grid references are shown on the map frame of each page.
Red figures denote the 100 km square and blue figures the 1 km square.
Example, page 4: Beverley Racecourse 502 440

The reference can also be written using the National Grid two-letter prefix shown on this page, where 5 and 4 are replaced by TA to give TA0240.

4.2 inches to 1 mile   **Scale of main map pages**   **1:15,000**

0		1/4	miles	1/2		3/4		1
0	1/4		1/2	kilometres	3/4	1	1 1/4	1 1/2

Junction 9	Motorway & junction
Services	Motorway service area
	Primary road single/dual carriageway
Services	Primary road service area
	A road single/dual carriageway
	B road single/dual carriageway
	Other road single/dual carriageway
	Minor/private road, access may be restricted
← ←	One-way street
	Pedestrian area
	Track or footpath
	Road under construction
	Road tunnel
P	Parking
P+	Park & Ride
	Bus/coach station
	Railway & main railway station
	Railway & minor railway station
⊖	Underground station
⊖	Light railway & station
+++++++++	Preserved private railway

LC	Level crossing
●—●—●—●	Tramway
– – – – –	Ferry route
....	Airport runway
–·–·–·–	County, administrative boundary
▾▾▾▾▾▾▾	Mounds
I7	Page continuation 1:15,000
3	Page continuation to enlarged scale 1:10,000
	River/canal, lake, pier
	Aqueduct, lock, weir
465 ▲ Winter Hill	Peak (with height in metres)
	Beach
	Woodland
	Park
	Cemetery
	Built-up area
	Industrial/business building
	Leisure building
	Retail building
	Other building

⊓⊓⊓⊓⊓	City wall	♜	Castle
A&E	Hospital with 24-hour A&E department	🏛	Historic house or building
PO	Post Office	Wakehurst Place (NT)	National Trust property
📖	Public library	🏛	Museum or art gallery
i	Tourist Information Centre	🦅	Roman antiquity
i	Seasonal Tourist Information Centre	⊥	Ancient site, battlefield or monument
⛽⛽	Petrol station, 24 hour Major suppliers only	▄▄▄	Industrial interest
†	Church/chapel	❋	Garden
🚻	Public toilets	◉	Garden Centre Garden Centre Association Member
♿	Toilet with disabled facilities	♣	Garden Centre Wyevale Garden Centre
PH	Public house AA recommended	🌲🌲	Arboretum
🍴	Restaurant AA inspected	🛒	Farm or animal centre
Madeira Hotel	Hotel AA inspected	🦌	Zoological or wildlife collection
🎭	Theatre or performing arts centre	🦜	Bird collection
🎥	Cinema	🐋	Nature reserve
⚑	Golf course	🐟	Aquarium
▲	Camping AA inspected	V	Visitor or heritage centre
🚐	Caravan site AA inspected	🏉	Country park
▲🚐	Camping & caravan site AA inspected	⌒	Cave
🎢	Theme park	🏛	Windmill
🏰	Abbey, cathedral or priory	🛢	Distillery, brewery or vineyard

Beverley Racecourse

A1035

York Road

A1035

Willow Gv

Pasture

Tiger La

Waltham

Wood

Lane

Newbegin

4

New Pits

Westwood Hospital

Westwood Road

Woodlands

Crown Works

Albert

St. Giles's Ct

Bishops

Surg

Westwood

Road

Walkington

Champney Rd

Ellerker Rd

Central Avenue

Beverley Minster CE Prim Sch

Thrs Road

Greyfriars Crs

Golf Course

Beverley 20

Beverley 20

Beverley 20

Keldgate Road

B1230 Cartwright Lane

Grosvenor Pl

Sloe Lane

Admiral Walker Road

B1230 KE

Queensgate

A164

Butt La

Newton

Shorthill Hagg

Walkington Road

Beverley & East Riding Golf Club

Beverley Boys Grammar School

Cem

Cem

Victoria Road

Keldgate Shopping Cen

Ripon

Lincoln Avenue

Chester Avenue

Shepherd

3

Works

Poplars

Poplars Way

Yeoman Drive

Richmond Way

Princess Wy

Lincoln Way

St Johns Ct

Broadgate Farm

B1230

George Lane

Megson Way

Haven

Broadgate

Megson Way

Normandy Avenue

Queensmead

Alexandra Drive

Works

Shprds Lea

Thyme Way

4

Hayward Close

Colleridge GV

Browns Yard Ind Est

Wingfield Way

A164

Glenfield

A1079

Shepherd Lane

5

437

Butt Farm

502

03

A1079

164

A1079

Beverley 20

Westwood

Beverley 20

I grid square represents 500 metres

A B C D

E F G H

Meaux Road 10 11

Foxholme

Common Lane
Bridge

Woody
Carr

I

Lane

Common

Wawne

Lane

37

Fairholme La Cm La

Common

Street

Oarlam
Hill·Farm

2

Church La

Sutton

St Peter's Walk

Crofts Drain

Road

Holderness Drain

East Riding of Yorkshire

Carlam Lane

Cumbrian Way

3

Carlam Lane

Welshpool Cl

Cumbrian Way

Snowdon Way

Fairbourne Close

Kentmere

Aberdovey Cl

Av Cl

Ay Cl

A Cl

Kingston upon Hull

36

The Dales
Primary
School

Brm Cl

Horton
House Sch

Rtw

Snowdon Way

Portmadoc

Furness

Flkr Cl

Crss

Crsswd

**South
Field**

HU7

Harlech Cl

Common

Lothian Way

Lthm

Lthm

Lthm

Pennine Way

Wawne Ld

Bortck Cl

Gifford Close

S Cl

Wawne

Arncliffe Wy

Kettlewell Cl

Rishworth

Bortwick Cl

Bortck Rd

A Cl

Gifford

Gifford

Highlands
Health
Centre

4

Trawden
Close

Grampian Way

PO

Oldmain Drain

Thurlstone
Cl

Grampian
Shop Cen

Highlands
Primary
School

Greygarth
Cl

Road

Moorfoot
Cl

Rangely

Helvellyn
Cl

**Broadacre
Primary
School**

Kinderscout

Pennine

W Cl

Dalkeith

Foredyke Stream

5

Bownmoor
Wy

B Wy

C Cl

Ssngtn Cn

Whitehope Cl

Pyk Cl

Dalkeith

Blckhll

Blckwtr

Kibrdl Cl

Brecon

Frmm

Grantham Av

Wd Cl

Raucby

Pendle Cl

Way

Redmire
Cl

Ladyside
Cl

Cumbrian Way

435

Kesteven Wy

Pnnyhlm

Noseley

Highfd Grove

Emberton

Sapperton
Close

Saddleworth

Sedgebrook

Kingsbury

Brandon Way

Grove

E F I4 G H

Kesteven Foredyke Kingswood
College of Arts

Wawne Road

Hartsholme park

Tollymore Pk

Marbury park

Noddle Hill Way

Abingdon
Garth

Binbrook
Garth

Cosford garth

Bransholme

Bragdate Pk

Wawne Drain

Wawne Road

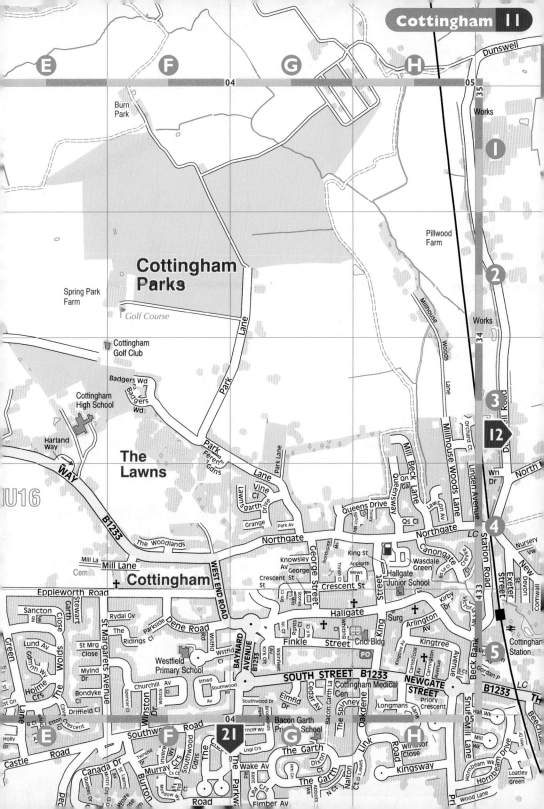

High
Bransholme

E   F   G   H

12

13

35

Swine Church Drain

I

Castle
Hill

Holderness Drain

North Carr

Whisperwood
Way

Briarwood

Honley

Wolsey Hill Way

Ellson Hills

Leadhills
Wy

Noddle Hill Way

Manston Garth

Leeming

Dwinnhill

Leadhills Way

Castlehill Road

Hornsea Rail Trail & Trans Pennine Trail

2

34

-holme

Avenue

Biggin

Okngtn Grth

Biggin Av

Suttoncross Drain

Goldcrest
Close

Biggin Hill
Prim Sch

Curlew

Kestrel

Lapwing Cl

Housemartin
Drive

Sittingbourne
Close

Rainham
Close

Canterbury
Drive

Carr
House

3

16

st. Riding o...

ngston upon

Scampton Garth

Topcliffe Garth

Noddle Hill Way

Lagoon Dr

Fulmar

Merlin

Blossom Gv

Acorn Gv

Deal
Close

Whitstable
Close

Higham
Close

Ramsgate Cl

Danby

4

Wawne Road

Mullion

Astral Gdns

Astral Way

Foxholme Rd

Avenue

Finch

Linnet

Howdale

Wysteria

Way

Crosmont

Greenhow

Ingleby Cl

Stornaway

Square

East Carr Road

Newlyn Cl

Logan Close

Truro Cl

Robdr

Astral Way

St James Close

Oaktree Dr

Road

Close

Maryan

Road

Lunedale Cl

Dunvegan Road

Stromness Way

Dressay

Gleneagles

Park

Golf Course

Leads Road

B1237

Robson Way

Surgery

Works

B1237 ROBSON WAY

Langsett Rd

Church

Street

Fossdale

Sutton Ct

Spring
Cottage
Prim Sch

Dalsetter Rise

PO

Gleneagles

5

Sutton Park
Golf Club

The
Fairways

B1237

Highfield

Highfield Close

Watson

College Street

Priestgate

Saltshouse Road

Church
St

SALTSHOUSE ROAD

Barra

Hamilton

B1237

Clear Vw

SALTSHOUSE

Dorchester Road

Broadstone Cl

Tweendykes
School

Limetree Av

The Lawns

Lowgate

Balham Avenue

Northolt Cl

Brockley

Epping

Bellfield

Avenue

Battersea

Lambwath
Prim Sch

Tween

Dykes

Road

Kingfisher Rise

Neasden
Primary School

Bayswater
Court

Fnch Cl

**Sutton-
on-Hull**

Sutton Road

Ings Road

Bellfield

Ealing Cl

12

13

Chelsea

Barking

Sutton

16

A · B · C · D

513 · 35 · 14

Swine Lane
Swine Church Drain
Swine South Side Drain

Gravel Hill Farm

1

2

a Rail Trail & Trans Pennine Trail

The Marrs

Low Farm
Low Farm Rd
Ganstead Lane

34

3

15
Carr House

East Riding of Yorkshire
Kingston upon Hull

Ganstead Drain

Ganstead Lane
A165
GANSTEAD LANE

Beckington Close

4

Frome Road
Welland Road
Buckland Close
Wansbeck Rd
Hardington Close
Holcombe Close
Wansbeck Road
Wansbeck Prim Sch
Eastmount Recreation Centre
Ellingham Close
Road
Tamar Gv
Shannon Road
Surg

5

Gleneagles
Park A33
Golf Course
Sutton Park Golf Club
Clear Vw
Lambwath Prim Sch
Bearwood Cl
Sandmoor Cl
Western Gailes Way
Augusta Close
Brent Avenue
Ebor
Duddon Gv
Shannon
Waveney
Kyle
Plym Gv
Longhill Primary School
St Mrgts Ct
PO
Cncl Bldg
Hodder Gv
Torridge
Kennet Road
Medina Road
Douglas Road
Arreton Close
Thanet Primary Sch
BILTO
Broad

SALTSHOUSE 513
The Princess Royal Hospital
Western Gailes Wy
Chelmer Road
14

A · B · **26** · C · D

ROAD
Harleston Cl
Alwoodley Close
Tweed
Avenue
HOLDERNESS ROAD
A165
Tedworth Road
Caledon

grid square represents 500 metres

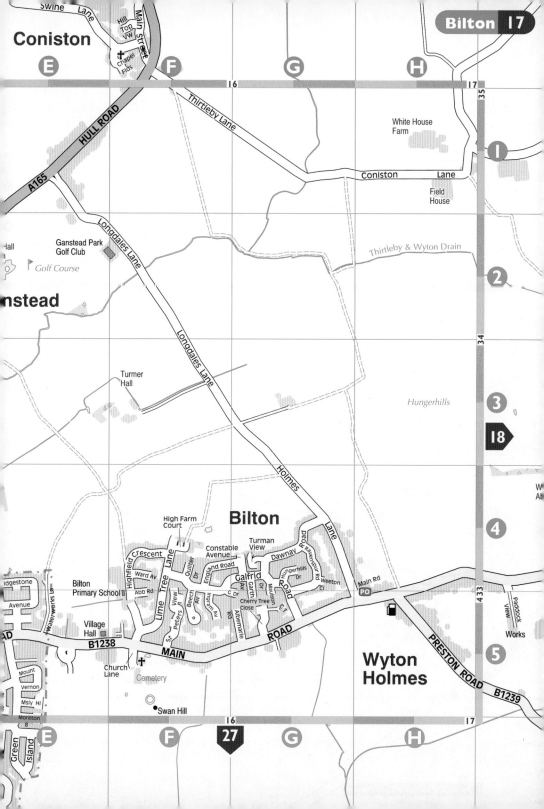

Coniston

E   F   G   H

16   17   35

I

Swine Lane
Hill Top Vw
Main Street
Chapel Flds

Thirtleby Lane

HULL ROAD
A165

White House Farm

Coniston Lane

Field House

Hall

Ganstead Park Golf Club

Golf Course

Longdales Lane

nstead

Thirtleby & Wyton Drain

2

34

Turmer Hall

Longdales Lane

Hungerhills

3

18

Holmes

High Farm Court

Bilton

Highfield Crescent
Lime Tree Lane
Quilter Dr
Constable Avenue
Turman View
England Road
Dawnay Road
Ravenspur Rd
Hungerhills Dr
Weeton Cl
Main Rd
PO

Ward Av
Abb Rd
St Peters View
Beech Av
Ingram Av
Albemarle Rd
Galfrid
G Dr
Garth
Av
Cherry Tree Close
Maulson Dr
C Dr
Road

4

433

Paddock View

Works

Bilton Primary School

Village Hall

B1238

Waterworks La

Idgestone
Avenue

RD

Mount Vernon
Msly Hl
Moreton B

Green Island

Church Lane

MAIN   ROAD

Cemetery

Swan Hill

Wyton Holmes

PRESTON ROAD
B1239

5

E   F   27   G   H

16   17

18

A   B   C   D

517   18

35

House

I

Lane

Field
House

Thirtleby

Bee
We

Spro

Wyton Drain

2

34

Jungerhill

3

◄ **17**

Brandywell

*Wyton
Park*

Wyton
Abbey

4

†

Wyton

B1238

433

Paddock
View

Works

Wyton
Holmes

5

PRES...N ROAD

B1239

517

517   18

A   B   ▼**28**   C   D

Wyton   Drain

I grid square represents 500 metres

*Preston
Field*

Pasture

E **F** **G** **H**

20 MOOR LANE B1238 21

Long L

35 Moor Farm

Hall Road

Mill Road

Raleigh Dr

B1238

Road

Cnst Cl

Harrison

Callands Rd

Chestnut Gv

The Green

Ash Close

PO

Plum Tree Road

Balk La

Church Lane

Sproatley Endowed Primary School

Boggle Lane

W Rd

I

2

34

3

SPROATLEY ROAD

B1240

Sproatley Grange

4

Humbleton Road

433

Humbleton Road

5

Nuttles Drain

North Farm

Nuttles Hall Farm

Lelley

E **F** **G** **H**

20 21

▼ **29**

Newfield Lane

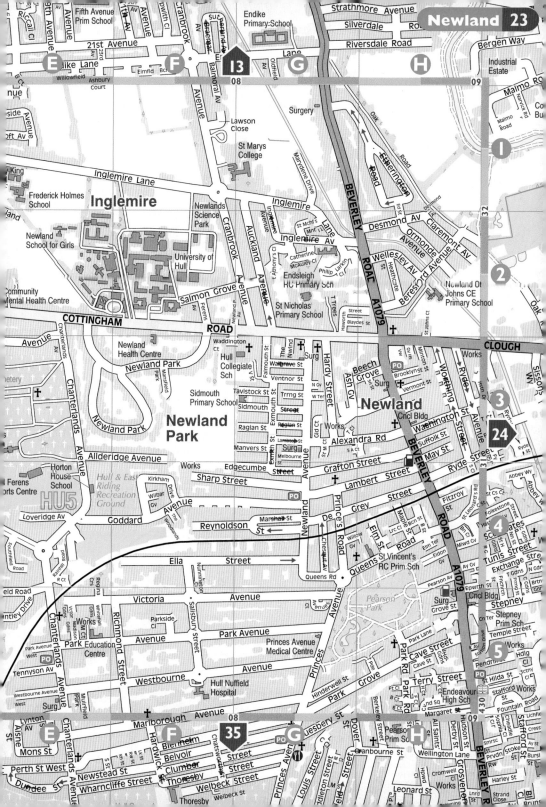

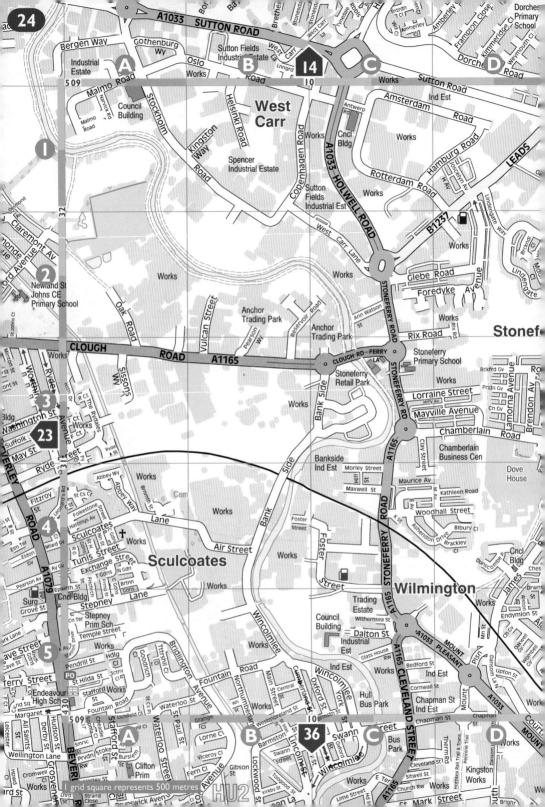

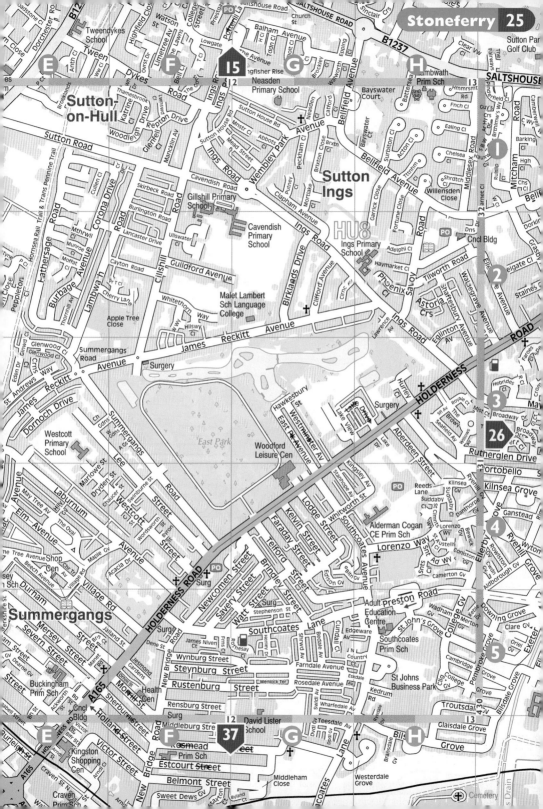

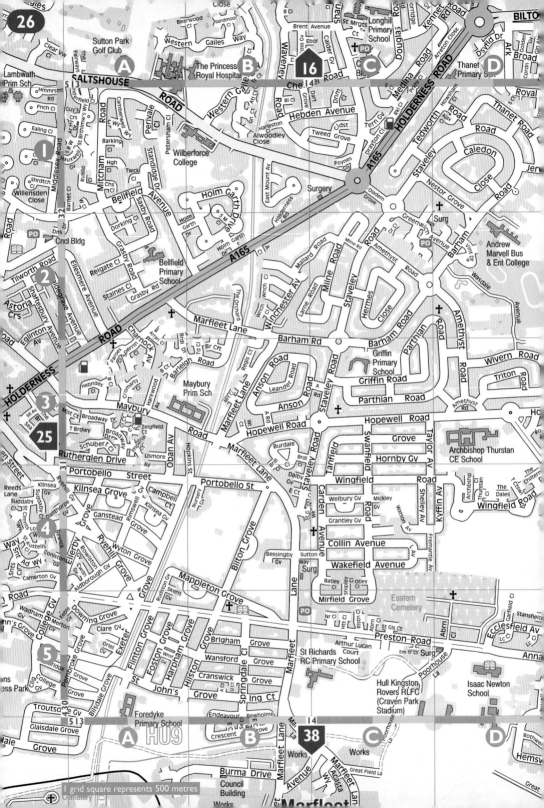

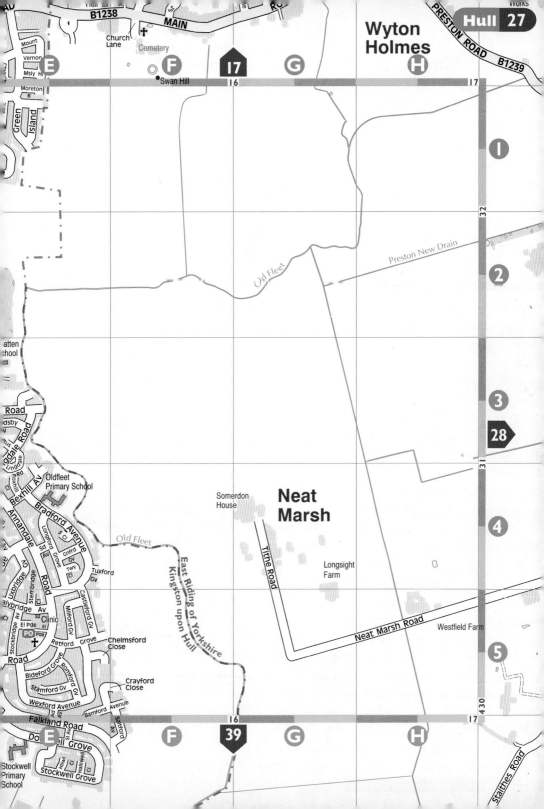

B1238

MAIN

PRESTON ROAD B1239

Wyton Holmes

Works

Church Lane

Cemetery

Mount Vernon

Msly Hl

Moreton B

E

F

17

G

H

Swan Hill

16

17

Green Island

1

32

Preston New Drain

Old Fleet

2

atten hool

Road

dsby

gdale Road

ngdale

Road

3

28

31

Oldfleet Primary School

Bexhill Av

Annandale

Bradford Avenue

Road

Longford Grove

Sd Av

Gnfrd Gv

TWY Cl

Somerdon House

Neat Marsh

4

Old Fleet

Tuxford Gv

East Riding of Yorkshire

Kingston upon Hull

Tithe Road

Longsight Farm

Uxbridge Gv

Stembridge

Castleford Gv

Milford Gv

lybridge Av

El Pde El

PO Pde

Retford Grove

Chelmsford Close

Stockbridge

Road

Bideford Grove

Romford Gv

Stamford Gv

Crayford Close

Neat Marsh Road

Westfield Farm

5

430

Wexford Avenue

Bamford Avenue

Stafford Av

Falkland Road

16

17

E

F

39

G

H

Staithes Road

Do well Grove

Stockwell Primary School

Stockwell Grove

Hllw

Hallwll

Nuttles Drain

North Farm

E

F

19 uttles all Farm

20

G

Lelley **H**

Humbleton

Newfield Lane

I

32

2

WAILEY ROAD

Nuttles Lane

Lelley Road

Duck Hill Well

East End

Lund Garth

New York

East End Road

3

31

Wrawby Lane

Cemetery

East End Road

Preston

Highfield Rd

Carputt

Ellis Cl

Grassam

Hunter Cl

Manor Park

Rands Est

Watkinson

Close

Addison Rd

Bartlett Cl

4

21

Weghill Road

5

430

reston mary Sch

South Holderness Sport ntre

E

South Holderness Technology College

F

41 ands rm

20

Weghill Road

G

Littl **H** **Weghill**

21

A   B   C   D

497   98

Wauldby
Scrogs

Wauldby Manor
Farm

Little
Wauldby Farm

1

2

Welton
Wold
Farm

Stonepit Road

Stonepit Road

Melton Bottom

3

Stonepit Road

Welton
Wold

4

45

5

Mill Road

Bow Road

Melton Bottom

Beverley 20

Works

497   98

A   B   46   C   D

Wolds Way & Bever

Trinity

1 grid square represents 500 metres

Trinity House Fa

Swanland Dale

Riplin

West Green

Elveley Drive

The Fairway

We
Ell

The Meadows

West Ella Rd

Manor Fields

Chapel La

Manor Court

West Ella Road

A164

Field Farm

Swanland Dale

Westwinds

Occupation Lane

Works

Dale Road

nd Dale

Occupation Lane

Beech Hill Road

Swanland

Northdale Park

N P

The Green

Wauldby View

Wood View

St Barnabas Drive

S B D

Easenby Cl

Westdale

Welton

Wld Vw

Gallands Cl

Meadow Cl

Dale Road

The Spinney

Northfield

Northfield

Fer Rise

Main Street

Paddock

Greenacres

Greenstiles Lane

Sykes

Crowther Way

Walk

Chantry

Dale East

Mere Way

Priory Cl

C W E

St Mary's

Beech Gr

Styles Croft

West Field Farm

Chantry Way

Queensour Way

St Mary's Mnt

North Drive

Hall Park

Styles Croft

Rise

West Field Lane

Surgery

On Hill

St Michael's

Stratton Park

Todds Close

West End

PO

Kemp Rd

Swanland Prim Sch

B1231

TRANBY LANE

Manor Road

The Park

Humber View

Humberl Cl

W Wold

Copper Beech Close

Kemp Road

West Levs Park

West

Grange Pk

Grange Farm

Humber Dale

Jenny Brough Lane

47

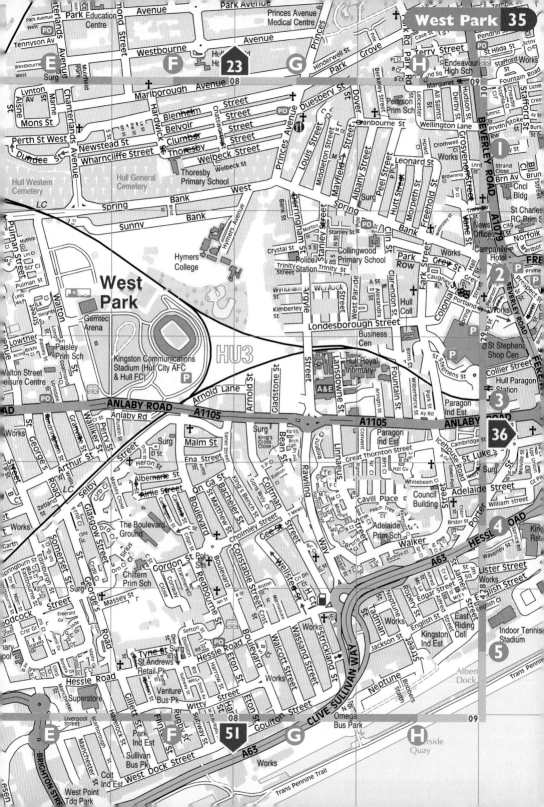

KINGSTON
UPON HULL

1 grid square represents 500 metres

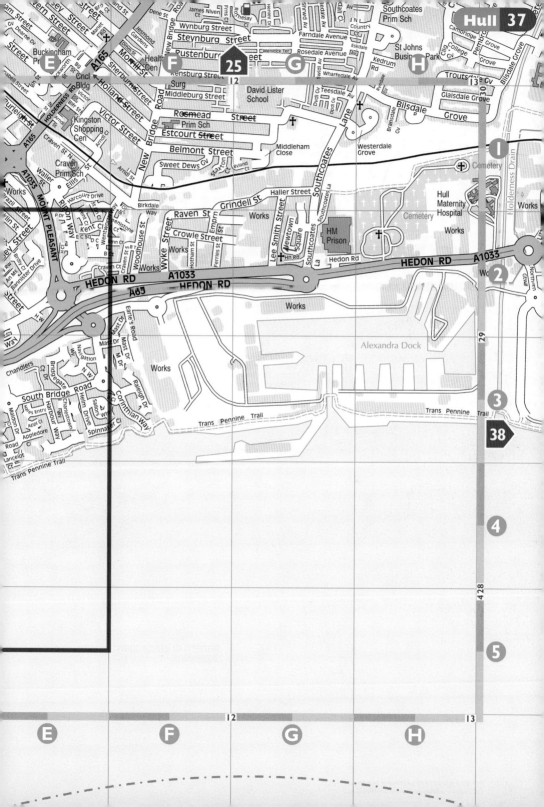

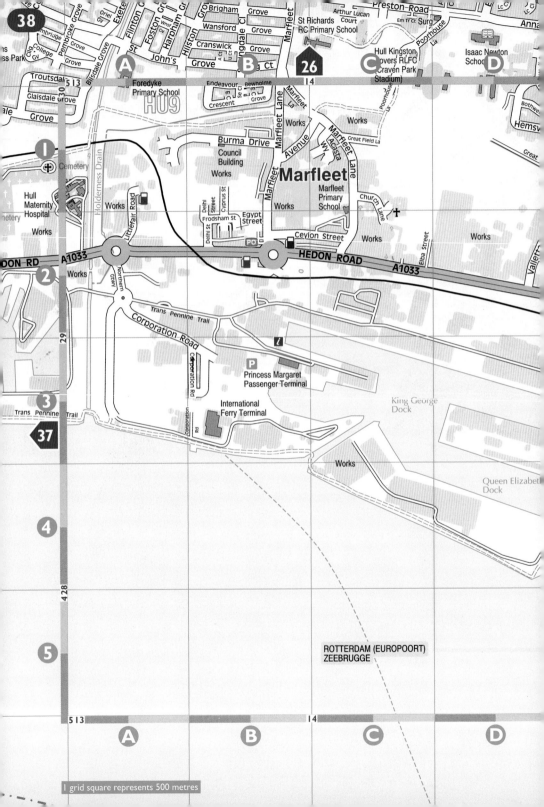

Weghill Road

E

F

29
20

G

H

South Holderness
Sports Centre

South Holderness
Technology
College

Rands
Farm

Weghill Road

Little Weghill

21

30

I

Wranglands

attocks Lane

HU12

Magdalen
House

2

Ha

e Park

Clough Garth

B1362

erry Tree La

MAIN STREET   **B1362**

29

Hedon

Forkerleys

3

MAGDALEN LANE

Brevere Road

Albina
Garth

Beck
Garth

Haven

Guy Garth

Poultney Crt

Brevere
Rd

Duncombe
Court

Allison Garth

Chapelry
Garth

St A Dr

St Anthony's Pk

Fewson
Garth

Inmans
Road

Watson

Fleet
Garth

Holcroft
Garth

Alured Garth

Oast Garth

Greville Road

Villier
Ct

Darrell Ct

Garth

Adeliza Grth

St Nicholas Gate

C St

Charles Street

Inmans
Primary
School

St Mary's Drive

Kirkholme

B Ct

Bond Street

St Michael's Drive

4

Acklam
Road

Hildyard Cl

Ainslie Rd

Andersons

Brkl

Stockholm

Havmer Drive

Cromwell Rd

Tailfer Rd

K C

W

Burstwick Drain

B1240

Mndr Cl

Chayt Dr

Waterland

Cleeve Road

Ainslie Rd

C R

TW

Shoemaker

S Cl

C W

Cavdy

Tennyson

C Rd

Emwy

Bgn Ct

5

Wyntryngm

Brn Wy

Sacred Gate

Dam

THORN ROAD

B1240

Cleeve
Road

Stockholm
Hill Farm

Ryhill Drain

E A1033

F

G

H

North Carr Drain

20

21

Thorn
Villa

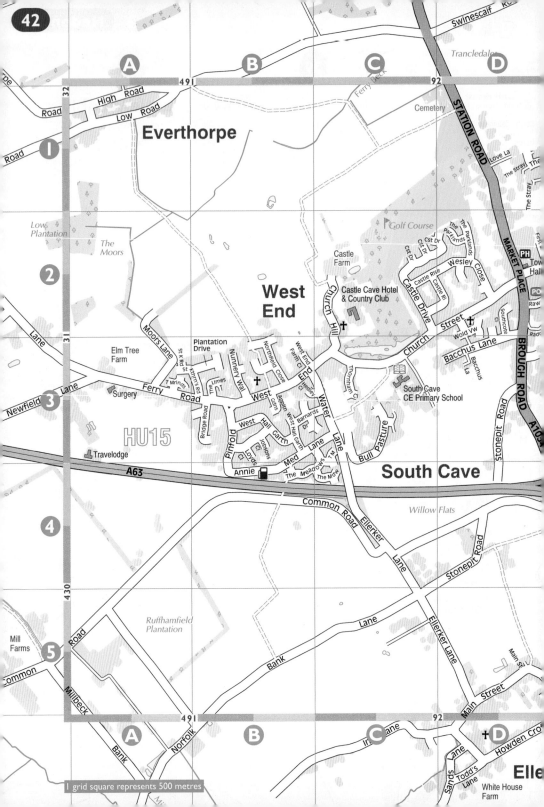

42

A   B   C   D

491   92

Everthorpe

Swinescaif

Trancledales

Cemetery

High Road

Low Road

Road

STATION ROAD

Love La

The Stray

The

1

Low Plantation

The Moors

Golf Course

The Parklands

Cst Dr

Cst Dr

MARKET PLACE

PH

Tow Hall

PO

2

Castle Farm

Castle Cave Hotel & Country Club

Castle Rise

Castle Ri

Castle Dr

Castle Drive

Wesley Close

Southcote

BROUGH ROAD

A10

Raw

West End

Church Hill

Church Street

Wold Vw

Bacchus Lane

Bacchus La

Bacchus

Lane

St K Rd

Moors Lane

Plantation Drive

Northfield close

West End Farm Cl

End

Thornham Cl

South Cave CE Primary School

Elm Tree Farm

Nunnery Wa

K'rm's Rd

T M'rln's

Limes Ct

Bedley

Water Lane

Lane

Ferry Road

Surgery

Bridge Road

Laplin

West Hall Garth

Jdns

Newfield

HU15

3

West Hall Garth

Pinfold

Jobsons

Loyds

Barnards

Med Lane

Bull Pasture

Annie

The Meadows

TM

The Mow

Travelodge

A63

South Cave

Common Road

Willow Flats

Ellerker Lane

Stonepit Road

4

Ruffhamfield Plantation

Lane

Ellerker Lane

Main St

Mill Farms

Road

Bank

Main Street

5

Millbeck

Common

491   92

Bank

Norfolk

A   B   Ir   C   Lane   D

Sands Lane

Todd's Lane

Howden Cro

Elle

White House Farm

1 grid square represents 500 metres

E F G H

Plantation

Great Wold Plantation

93 94 32

Wolds Way & High

Wold Lane

The Stray
Stray
The Stray

Little Wold

B Rd
S W
The Lea
Steep Hill

B Rd
Plum Tree Walk
Cleaves
Av
everley

Road

Fields

I

2

31

Mount Airy Farm

Ryeland Hill

Cliffs Plantation

Ellerker North Wold

Wolds Way & High Hunsley Circuit

3

Woodale Farm

Wol Farm

Ellerker Wold Lane

Bilks Hill

4

A63

Hunsdale Farm

430

✝

Wolds Way & High Hunsley Circuit

Ilerke Beck

Hall Farm

Spout

Hill

5

Ring Beck Lane

A63

Burrill Lane

Dale Road

Wandell's View

Brantingham

93 94

E F G **Brantingham**

Thorpe

PO

The Outgang

New

Crook Hill

E F G H

96 Welton Dale 97

Elloughton Dale

Stonepit Road

Beverley 20

Wolds Way

I

28 30

Elloughton Wold

High Road

ughton

2

Elloughton Hill

Welton Mill

Mill Pond

Wolds Way

Bow Road

Hall Walk

Kidd Lane

Dale Road

Crossall Hill La

Wolds Way & Beverley 20

A63

Beverley 20

Chapel Hill

Welton

Holly Hill

Temple

T C

Bartrams

Cowgate

Church St

St Anns Walk

Welton Old

Temple Close

Temple La

3

Beckside

Creyke Lane

Park Rd

St Helen's Drive

St Annes School

Melton

Road

Broadacre Park

The Crescent

Park Rd

Cem

Road

East Dale Road

27

Robin Cl

River Crescent

Medlar Drive

Broadley Croft

Welton Primary School

Broadley Way

Low Field Lane

South Hunsley School

S   es

4

Aire

Wiske Av

As Wk

Frtld Vw

Meden

Loxley

Elloughtonthorpe

C Dr

E Cl

Ke Dr

Melton Old

Road

Reynolds Close

Swale Rd

Langthwaite

Poolbank Lane

Pool Bank Farm

46

Constable Cl

Hsthwte Rd

Husthwaite Rd

Airthrpe Crs

Ling Cl

Works

Gibson La South

Way

Millias Cl

Common Lane

Pool Beck

Low Field Lane

Low Field Farm

5

426

LC

Monks (West

96 97

E F G H

Low Common

Gibson La Works

LC

Humber Ind Est

River Humber

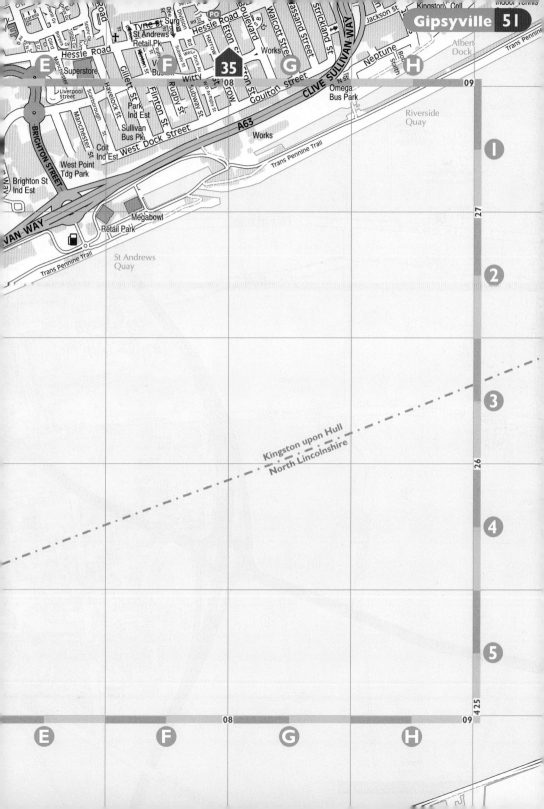

Chowder Ness

Best Western Reeds Hotel

Far Ings National Nature Reserve

Visitors Centre

Far Ings Lane

Far Ings Road

Works

Humber Bridge

Council Building

WATERSIDE ROAD

Bh La

Far Ings Road

B1218

Works

Clapson's La

Hewson's La

Dam Road

Stable Lane

Humber Road

Stable Lane

Ramblers Lane

Haven Rd

Vagarth

Victoria Drive

Road

Works

Council Terrace

Dam Road

Gravel-Pit Road

Westfield House

West Acridge

West Grove

Ponds Wy

Shadwell Rise

Castledyke Prim Sch

CASTLEDYKE WEST

FLEETGATE B1218

Westfield Road

Westfield Road

Westfield Road

Western Dr

Regency Ct

Hill Dr

Works

Duncan Dr

Sur

Green Gate

Birch Wood Close

P Ct

Riverbank Rise

C Ct

WC

W Ct

Elder Cl

Humber View

Heron

Teal Dr

Hessle View

Feyzin Dr

Furniss Court

Sunnybank

A1077 FERRIBY ROAD

Harrowdyke

Ramsden Av

Cliff Grove

Providence

Grange Av

DN18

Warrendale

Bradwell Cl

Tofts Rd

Milson Cl

Road

Cncl Bldg

Lunn's Crs

Crescent

Bowmandale

Pelham Cl

G G Ct

Forkedale

Pitman Av

Warwick Drive

M Ct

N Ct

Millfields

Bowmandale Prim Sch

Bowmandale

RIBY ROAD

Coddard Cl

A D

A Dr

Varah Close

Appleyard Dr

Goddard Cl

Tofts

Summerdale

Harvest Avenue

Stevenson's Wy

Webb Close

Sharpe Cl

Wn Cl

Horkstow Road

Green Gate

Barton Grange

1 grid square represents 500 metres

DN18

E   F   G   H

04   05

Barton Waterside

North

LC

I

2

Pasture Road

Lane

Falkland Way

Victory Way

South Humberside Industrial Estate

Nursery Cl

Lower Mdw

Harriet Road

Pasture Road Sth

Humber Bridge Industrial Estate

Antelope Road

Ardent Rd

Pasture Rd South

South Marsh Farm

Barton-on-Humber Station

Butts

St Peters Orch

Marsh Sqs

Pasture Road

Greenway

W Wy   Treece Gardens

East Gv

Willow Drive

Barton- upon-Humber

Falkland Way

3

54

Queen's Av

St Peters Cl

Barton St Peters CE Primary School

Works

East

Acridge

Saxon

Norman Close

Barrow Road Cemetery

New Options Barton School

22

Tysons Cl

Queen St

Ct St

King St

Soutergate

PO   Pol Stn

Burgate

St M'y Lane

Beck Hill

Green Lane

Church View

Whitecross Street

Priestgate

Mrkt Pl

MARKET PLACE   **A1077**

BARROW   **ROAD**   **A1077**

ROAD

Castledyke South

Castle Ct

Preston La

Baysgarth Lower School

Baysgarth School

Nightingale Cl

Stphn Crs

Highfnd Crs

Quen Dane

Cornhill Dr

Glebe Way

Cornhill Farm

4

Calstor Rd

Calstor Road

Stowgarth

Swimming Pool

The Bridges

Baysgarth Leisure Centre   Curtis Close

Park View

Lodge Av

Hawthorn Ga

Eastfield

Meadow Drive

Nicolson Drive

River View

Kingston View

Blythe Ct

Lincoln Drive

Fairfield Drive

Princess Dr

421

5

Beech Grove

E   F   G   H

04   05

54

A B C D

5 05 06

23

I

†

Barrow Haven

West Hann Lar

The Castles
● (Motte & Baileys)

West Marsh Lane

The Be

2

Ferry Road

New Options
Barton School

A1077

3

A1077

B1

FERRY

Ferry Road

◄ **53**

22

Barrow Mere

Harvest Rd

The Brambles

Rowan Hedgerow Cl

Chestnut

FERRY ROAD

Schofield Cl Millfield

Mill La

BARTON LANE

Barrow RFC

4

Beech Grove

Highfields

Blacksmith

Ferry Road

Silver Street

Orchard Cl

5

Westoby Lane

Park View

421

Barrow Hall

Beech Garth

5 05 06

A B C D

Calstor Road

B1206

I grid square represents 500 metres

USING THE STREET INDEX

Street names are listed alphabetically. Each street name is followed by its postal town or area locality, the Postcode District, the page number, and the reference to the square in which the name is found.

Standard index entries are shown as follows:

1st Av HULLN HU6 .... 13 F5

Street names and selected addresses not shown on the map due to scale restrictions are shown in the index with an asterisk:

Ada Holmes Cir HULLN HU6 * 13 E5

GENERAL ABBREVIATIONS

ACC ....ACCESS	CTYD ....COURTYARD	HLS ....HILLS	MWY ....MOTORWAY	SE ....SOUTH EAS
ALY ....ALLEY	CUTT ....CUTTINGS	HO ....HOUSE	N ....NORTH	SER ....SERVICE ARE
AP ....APPROACH	CV ....COVE	HOL ....HOLLOW	NE ....NORTH EAST	SH ....SHOR
AR ....ARCADE	CYN ....CANYON	HOSP ....HOSPITAL	NW ....NORTH WES	SHOP ....SHOPPIN
ASS ....ASSOCIATION	DEPT ....DEPARTMENT	HRB ....HARBOUR	O/P ....OVERPASS	SKWY ....SKYWA
AV ....AVENUE	DL ....DALE	HTH ....HEATH	OFF ....OFFICE	SMT ....SUMM
BCH ....BEACH	DM ....DAM	HTS ....HEIGHTS	ORCH ....ORCHARD	SOC ....SOCIET
BLDS ....BUILDINGS	DR ....DRIVE	HVN ....HAVEN	OV ....OVAL	SP ....SPU
BND ....BEND	DRO ....DROVE	HWY ....HIGHWAY	PAL ....PALACE	SPR ....SPRIN
BNK ....BANK	DRY ....DRIVEWAY	IMP ....IMPERIAL	PAS ....PASSAGE	SQ ....SQUAR
BR ....BRIDGE	DWGS ....DWELLINGS	IN ....INLET	PAV ....PAVILION	ST ....STREE
BRK ....BROOK	E ....EAST	IND EST ....INDUSTRIAL ESTATE	PDE ....PARADE	STN ....STATIO
BTM ....BOTTOM	EMB ....EMBANKMENT	INF ....INFIRMARY	PH ....PUBLIC HOUSE	STR ....STREA
BUS ....BUSINESS	EMBY ....EMBASSY	INFO ....INFORMATION	PK ....PARK	STRD ....STRAN
BVD ....BOULEVARD	ESP ....ESPLANADE	INT ....INTERCHANGE	PKWY ....PARKWAY	SW ....SOUTH WES
BY ....BYPASS	EST ....ESTATE	IS ....ISLAND	PL ....PLACE	TDG ....TRADIN
CATH ....CATHEDRAL	EX ....EXCHANGE	JCT ....JUNCTION	PLN ....PLAIN	TER ....TERRAC
CEM ....CEMETERY	EXPY ....EXPRESSWAY	JTY ....JETTY	PLNS ....PLAINS	THWY ....THROUGHWA
CEN ....CENTRE	EXT ....EXTENSION	KG ....KING	PLZ ....PLAZA	TNL ....TUNNE
CFT ....CROFT	F/O ....FLYOVER	KNL ....KNOLL	POL ....POLICE STATION	TOLL ....TOLLWA
CH ....CHURCH	FC ....FOOTBALL CLUB	L ....LAKE	PR ....PRINCE	TPK ....TURNPIK
CHA ....CHASE	FK ....FORK	LA ....LANE	PREC ....PRECINCT	TR ....TRAC
CHYD ....CHURCHYARD	FLD ....FIELD	LDG ....LODGE	PREP ....PREPARATORY	TRL ....TRA
CIR ....CIRCLE	FLDS ....FIELDS	LGT ....LIGHT	PRIM ....PRIMARY	TWR ....TOWE
CIRC ....CIRCUS	FLS ....FALLS	LK ....LOCK	PROM ....PROMENADE	U/P ....UNDERPAS
CL ....CLOSE	FM ....FARM	LKS ....LAKES	PRS ....PRINCESS	UNI ....UNIVERSIT
CLFS ....CLIFFS	FT ....FORT	LNDG ....LANDING	PRT ....PORT	UPR ....UPPE
CMP ....CAMP	FTS ....FLATS	LTL ....LITTLE	PT ....POINT	V ....VAL
CNR ....CORNER	FWY ....FREEWAY	LWR ....LOWER	PTH ....PATH	VA ....VALLE
CO ....COUNTY	FY ....FERRY	MAG ....MAGISTRATE	PZ ....PIAZZA	VIAD ....VIADUC
COLL ....COLLEGE	GA ....GATE	MAN ....MANSIONS	QD ....QUADRANT	VIL VILL
COM ....COMMON	GAL ....GALLERY	MD ....MEAD	QU ....QUEEN	VIS ....VIST
COMM ....COMMISSION	GDN ....GARDEN	MDW ....MEADOWS	QY ....QUAY	VLG ....VILLAG
CON ....CONVENT	GDNS ....GARDENS	MEM ....MEMORIAL	R ....RIVER	VLS ....VILLA
COT ....COTTAGE	GLD ....GLADE	MI ....MILL	RBT ....ROUNDABOUT	VW ....VIE
COTS ....COTTAGES	GLN ....GLEN	MKT ....MARKET	RD ....ROAD	W ....WES
CP ....CAPE	GN ....GREEN	MKTS ....MARKETS	RDG ....RIDGE	WD ....WOO
CPS ....COPSE	GND ....GROUND	ML ....MALL	REP ....REPUBLIC	WHF ....WHAR
CR ....CREEK	GRA ....GRANGE	MNR ....MANOR	RES ....RESERVOIR	WK ....WAL
CREM ....CREMATORIUM	GRG ....GARAGE	MS ....MEWS	RFC ....RUGBY FOOTBALL CLUB	WKS ....WALK
CRS ....CRESCENT	GT ....GREAT	MSN ....MISSION	RI ....RISE	WLS ....WELL
CSWY ....CAUSEWAY	GTWY ....GATEWAY	MT ....MOUNT	RM ....RAMP	YD ....YAR
CT ....COURT	GV ....GROVE	MTN ....MOUNTAIN	RW ....ROW	YHA ....YOUTH HOSTE
CTRL ....CENTRAL	HGR ....HIGHER	MTS ....MOUNTAINS	S ....SOUTH	
CTS ....COURTS	HL ....HILL	MUS ....MUSEUM	SCH ....SCHOOL	

POSTCODE TOWNS AND AREA ABBREVIATIONS

ANL/KKEL ....Anlaby/Kirk Ella	BRAN ....Bransholme	CHULLS ....Central Kingston upon Hull south	HESSLE ....Hessle	SINGS ....Sutton Ings
ANLPK/PPK ....Anlaby Park/ Pickering Park	BRWUH ....Barrow-upon- Humber	CHULLW ....Central Kingston upon Hull west	HULLE ....Kingston upon Hull east	SPR/BIL ....Sproatley/Bilto
BEV ....Beverley	BTNUH ....Barton-upon-Humber	COT/SKID ....Cottingham/Skidby	HULLN ....Kingston upon Hull north	SUL/NEW ....Sulcoates/Newlan
BR/NC/SC ....Brough/North Cave/ South Cave	CHULLN ....Central Kingston upon Hull north	HEDON ....Hedon	NF/SW ....North Ferriby/Swanland	

Index - streets

1st - Alf

fred Av CHULLW HU3 * 35 E5
fred Gelder St CHULLS HU1 2 D3
fred St CHULLW HU3 35 H4
friston Cl BRAN HU7 14 D5
son Garth HEDON HU12 41 E3
anhall Wy ANL/KKEL HU10 32 B2
anson Dr COT/SKID HU16 22 B1
an V HULLE HU9 * 37 F1
deridge Av SUL/NEW HU5 23 E3
endale HULLE HU9 * 37 F1
erford Dr BRAN HU7 14 C2
erthorpe Crs
BR/NC/SC HU15 45 E5
iance Av CHULLW HU3 34 D2
iance La CHULLW HU3 34 D3
oa Cl HULLN HU6 13 F3
Saints Cl HESSLE HU13 49 E4
Saints Ms HEDON HU12 28 D4
Saints' St CHULLW HU3 35 H1
ma Av SUL/NEW HU5 * 24 A4
ma Cl ANL/KKEL HU10 32 D2
ma St HULLE HU9 3 G2
mond Gv CHULLW HU3 35 H3
pha Av BEV HU17 4 C3
ston Av SINGS HU8 24 D5
thorpe Rd BRAN HU7 13 H2
ured Garth HEDON HU12 41 E3
woodley Cl SINGS HU8 26 B1
nanda Cl HULLN HU6 12 D5
nberley Cl BRAN HU7 14 C5
nethyst Rd HULLE HU9 26 D2
npleforth Gv SUL/NEW HU5 34 A1
nsterdam Rd BRAN HU7 24 C1
nys Gv CHULLW HU3 * 34 D4
caster Av SUL/NEW HU5 22 C3
chor Rd HULLN HU6 13 G3
court HULLN HU6 12 C5
dersons Cl HEDON HU12 41 E5
drew La HEDON HU12 40 C4
laby Av ANLPK/PPK HU4 33 H3
laby House Est
ANL/KKEL HU10 [illegible]
laby Park Rd North
ANLPK/PPK HU4 33 H4
laby Park Rd South
ANLPK/PPK HU4 49 H2
laby Rd ANLPK/PPK HU4 34 A3
lafgate ANL/KKEL HU10 33 F3
nandale Rd ANL/KKEL HU10 32 B1
HULLE HU9 26 D5
ne St CHULLS HU1 2 B4
nie Med La BR/NC/SC HU15 42 B4
nie Reed Rd BEV HU17 5 H5
n Watson St BRAN HU7 24 C2
son Rd HULLE HU9 26 B3
telope Rd BTNUH DN18 53 G2
tholme Cl BRAN HU7 15 E5
twerp Rd BRAN HU7 24 C1
pin Cl BRAN HU7 9 G4
ple Cft COT/SKID HU16 10 B3
pledore Cl HULLE HU9 3 J4
plegarth Ms COT/SKID HU16 11 G4
plegarth Rd SINGS HU8 3 H1
pleton Gdns BR/NC/SC HU15 42 B3
pleton Rd SUL/NEW HU5 22 C4
ple Tree Cl SINGS HU8 25 E2
pletree Ms ANL/KKEL HU10 20 C5
ple Tree Wk COT/SKID HU16 12 B5
pleyard Dr BTNUH DN18 52 C5
chbishop Cl HULLE HU9 26 D4
con Dr ANLPK/PPK HU4 34 B3
den Ct SUL/NEW HU5 22 A4
den Rd BEV HU17 5 F4
dent Rd BTNUH DN18 53 G3
dmore Cl HULLE HU9 26 B2
gent Cl HULLN HU6 13 F3
gyle Av HULLE HU9 * 37 F1
gyle St CHULLW HU3 35 G2
kley Cl BR/NC/SC HU15 44 C5
k Royal SPR/BIL HU11 16 D5
lington Av COT/SKID HU16 11 H5
SUL/NEW HU5 * 35 E1
ington St CHULLW HU3 35 H3
mstrong Cl BEV HU17 7 F1
ncliffe Cl BRAN HU7 9 F4
ncliffe Wy COT/SKID HU16 21 G1
nold La CHULLW HU3 35 F3
nold St CHULLW HU3 35 G3
non Vls SUL/NEW HU5 * 24 A4
ram Gv HULLN HU6 22 C1
ran Cl HULLE HU9 26 A2
ras Dr COT/SKID HU16 21 E1
reton Cl SINGS HU8 16 D5
thur Lucan Ct HULLE HU9 26 C5
thur St CHULLW HU3 35 E4
undel Cl HULLE HU9 37 E1
undel St HULLE HU9 37 F1
cott Cl ANLPK/PPK HU4 34 B4
BEV HU17 4 D2
h Av BR/NC/SC HU15 44 D3
hbourne Gv CHULLW HU3 * 35 E4
hbrook SINGS HU8 * 24 D5
hburn Gv CHULLW HU3 * 35 E2
hbury Ct HULLN HU6 23 E1
hby Cl ANLPK/PPK HU4 33 H2
hby Rd ANLPK/PPK HU4 33 G5
h Cl BEV HU17 5 E3
HESSLE HU13 48 C1
SPR/BIL HU11 19 E2
hcombe Rd BRAN HU7 13 H2
hdale Pk NF/SW HU14 46 C3
h Dene BEV HU17 6 A4
hdene Cl ANL/KKEL HU10 33 E2
hdene Vls SINGS HU8 * 24 D5
h Dr ANL/KKEL HU10 33 F1
hendon Dr SINGS HU8 24 C4
hgate Rd ANL/KKEL HU10 21 E4
h Gv ANL/KKEL HU10 20 D5
CHULLW HU3 * 34 D4
SUL/NEW HU5 23 G3
hthorpe HULLN HU6 12 D3
hton Cl HULLN HU6 12 D3
hwell Av HULLE HU9 38 D1
hworth Dr ANL/KKEL HU10 20 B5
hworthy Cl BRAN HU7 14 A2
ke Ms SUL/NEW HU5 22 B3
kew Av ANLPK/PPK HU4 34 B5
pen Cl ANLPK/PPK HU4 50 A1
pen Wk BR/NC/SC HU15 45 E4
tley St CHULLW HU3 34 D2
Aston Hall Dr NF/SW HU14 46 D3
Aston Rd ANL/KKEL HU10 33 F1
Astoria Crs SINGS HU8 25 H2
Astral Cl BRAN HU7 15 F4
HESSLE HU13 49 F1
Astral Gdns BRAN HU7 15 E4
Astral Rd HESSLE HU13 49 F1
Astral Wy BRAN HU7 15 F4
Astwood Av HULLE HU9 39 E1
Athelstan Rd BEV HU17 5 E4
Athens Cl CHULLW HU3 34 D4
Athletic Gv CHULLW HU3 * 35 F4
Atholl Av HESSLE HU13 49 E1
Athol St CHULLW HU3 34 D4
Atkinson Dr BR/NC/SC HU15 44 C3
Atlanta Ct SINGS HU8 26 B1
Attringham Pk BRAN HU7 13 H1
Atwick Ct HULLE HU9 26 B5
Auburn Cl HULLE HU9 26 C5
Auckland Av HULLN HU6 23 G2
Audley St CHULLN HU2 36 A1
Augusta Cl SINGS HU8 16 B5
Augustines Ms HEDON HU12 40 D3
Augustine's Ms HEDON HU12 * 40 D3
Augustus Dr BR/NC/SC HU15 44 D4
Avenue Crs CHULLW HU3 * 35 F4
Avenue Halcyon HESSLE HU13 49 E2
Avenues Ct SUL/NEW HU5 23 G5
The Avenue ANL/KKEL HU10 32 C2
BRAN HU7 15 G5
CHULLW HU3 * 35 E4
COT/SKID HU16 * 11 G5
Avondale ANLPK/PPK HU4 49 H2
HULLE HU9 * 25 F5
Avondale Crs SUL/NEW HU5 * 35 E1
Avon St SINGS HU8 * 25 E5
Avon V HULLE HU9 * 37 G1
Axdane HULLN HU6 12 C4
Axholme Ct HULLE HU9 * 3 H5
Axminster Cl BRAN HU7 14 D3
Aylesbury Gv SUL/NEW HU5 34 B1
Aylesford Ct CHULLW HU3 35 F4
Aysgarth Av HULLN HU6 22 C2

B

Babington Rw HULLE HU9 * 37 E1
Bacchus La BR/NC/SC HU15 42 D3
Bacheler St CHULLW HU3 35 F4
Bacon Garth La COT/SKID HU16 21 G1
Baden Cl SUL/NEW HU5 23 H4
Badgers Wd COT/SKID HU16 11 F3
Bagby Ms SUL/NEW HU5 22 B3
Baildon Ct HEDON HU12 41 F4
Bailey La COT/SKID HU16 12 B3
Bainbridge Av HULLE HU9 26 D4
Bainton Cl BEV HU17 4 C4
Bainton Gv HULLN HU6 12 C5
Baker St CHULLS HU1 2 B2
Bakers Yd NF/SW HU14 * 46 D3
Bakewell Cl HULLE HU9 26 D5
Balfour Ldg HULLE HU9 * 37 E1
Balfour St HULLE HU9 37 E1
Balham Av SINGS HU8 15 G5
Balk La SPR/BIL HU11 19 E2
Balk Ms SUL/NEW HU5 22 B3
Ballantyne Cl BRAN HU7 25 E2
Ballathie Cl HULLN HU6 13 F2
Balmoral Av HULLN HU6 13 F5
Balmoral Dr BEV HU17 6 D3
Bamford Av HULLE HU9 27 E5
Bank Side SUL/NEW HU5 24 B4
Bank St CHULLW HU3 35 G1
Bannister Cl HESSLE HU13 49 E4
Bannister Dr HULLE HU9 3 J2
Bantock Garth ANLPK/PPK HU4 33 H5
Barbarry Rd HEDON HU12 40 B3
Barberry Ct BR/NC/SC HU15 44 D4
CHULLW HU3 35 G4
Bardshaw HULLN HU6 12 D3
Bargate Gv SUL/NEW HU5 34 B1
Barham Rd HULLE HU9 26 D2
Barkers Ml BEV HU17 7 G1
Barking Cl SINGS HU8 26 A1
Barkworth Cl ANL/KKEL HU10 33 F3
Barleigh Cft HULLE HU9 26 B3
Barleigh Rd HULLE HU9 26 A3
Barleyholme BEV HU17 7 G1
Barmouth Cl BRAN HU7 9 G3
Barmston Cl BEV HU17 5 G4
Barmston Rd BEV HU17 5 G4
Barmston St CHULLN HU2 36 B1
Barnards Dr BR/NC/SC HU15 42 B3
Barnard Wy HEDON HU12 41 E5
Barnes Cl BEV HU17 5 G5
Barnes Wy BRAN HU7 13 G2
Barnetby Rd HESSLE HU13 49 F1
Barnet Cl SINGS HU8 26 A1
Barnsley St SINGS HU8 24 D5
Barnstaple Rd BRAN HU7 14 D3
Baroness Cl HULLN HU6 13 F3
Barra Cl SINGS HU8 15 H5
Barraclough's La BTNUH DN18 52 D1
Barrick Cl BRWUH DN19 55 E4
Barrington Av SUL/NEW HU5 22 D3
Barrow Ct CHULLW HU3 23 H5
Barrow La HESSLE HU13 48 D2
Barrow Rd BRWUH DN19 55 G2
BTNUH DN18 53 G4
Bartlett Av BEV HU17 6 D1
Bartlett Cl HEDON HU12 29 E5
Barton Broads Pk
BTNUH DN18 * 53 E2
Barton Dr HESSLE HU13 48 D3
Barton La BRWUH DN19 54 D2
Barton St BRWUH DN19 55 E3
Bartrams BR/NC/SC HU15 45 F3
Basil Dr BEV HU17 6 D2
Bathurst St CHULLW HU3 35 H4
Batley Cl HULLE HU9 26 C4
Battersea Cl SINGS HU8 25 H1
Baxter Ga HEDON HU12 41 E3
Bay Ct BEV HU17 6 C4
Baynard Av COT/SKID HU16 11 G5
Baysdale BRAN HU7 14 B5
Bayswater Ct SINGS HU8 25 H1
Beacon Av BTNUH DN18 52 D4
Beacon Cl HESSLE HU13 49 E4
Beaconsfield Gdns
SUL/NEW HU5 * 23 G3
Beaconsfield St SUL/NEW HU5 23 H4
Beaconsfield Vls HULLE HU9 * 37 F1
Beadlam Ms SUL/NEW HU5 22 C2
Beamsley Wy BRAN HU7 9 E5
Bean St CHULLW HU3 35 G3
Bearwood Cl SINGS HU8 16 A5
Beaufort Cl CHULLW HU3 35 H3
Beaulieu Ct HULLE HU9 26 A3
Beaumont Ct HULLE HU9 3 K1
Beautiman Ct HULLN HU6 13 E5
Beaver Rd BEV HU17 5 G5
Beccles Cl SINGS HU8 16 B5
Beck Bank COT/SKID HU16 12 A5
Beckdale BRAN HU7 14 C5
Beck Garth HEDON HU12 41 E3
Beck Hl BTNUH DN18 53 E4
Beckhole Cl CHULLW HU3 35 E3
Beckington Cl SINGS HU8 16 C4
Beck La BRWUH DN19 55 E3
Beckside BEV HU17 7 F1
BR/NC/SC HU15 45 F3
Beckside Cl HULLN HU6 13 F4
Beckside North BEV HU17 7 G1
Beck View Rd BEV HU17 5 H5
Bedale Av HULLE HU9 25 G5
Bedale Ms BR/NC/SC HU15 44 D5
Bedford Rd HESSLE HU13 49 F1
Bedford St SINGS HU8 24 C5
Beech Av ANL/KKEL HU10 32 D1
BEV HU17 5 E3
HEDON HU12 40 C3
SINGS HU8 25 E4
SPR/BIL HU11 17 F5
Beechcliffe Av HULLN HU6 13 G4
Beech Cl CHULLW HU3 35 G4
SPR/BIL HU11 18 D1
Beechdale COT/SKID HU16 12 A5
Beech Dr NF/SW HU14 46 A3
The Beeches SUL/NEW HU5 * 23 G4
Beechfield HULLN HU6 13 F5
Beechfield Dr ANL/KKEL HU10 20 C4
Beech Garth BRWUH DN19 54 D5
Beech Gv CHULLW HU3 * 35 G4
HESSLE HU13 48 C1
NF/SW HU14 31 G4
SINGS HU8 * 24 C3
SUL/NEW HU5 23 G3
Beech Hill Rd NF/SW HU14 31 G3
Beech Lawn ANL/KKEL HU10 33 E3
Beech Rd BR/NC/SC HU15 44 C2
Beech Tree Cl BEV HU17 5 E2
Beeford Gv HULLN HU6 22 D1
Beilby St CHULLW HU3 34 D4
Belfry Ct SINGS HU8 16 B5
Belgrave Dr ANLPK/PPK HU4 34 B3
Bellamy Ct HULLE HU9 3 K1
Bell Cl BRAN HU7 15 F5
Bellfield Av SINGS HU8 25 H1
Bellfield Dr ANL/KKEL HU10 20 D5
Bells Rd HEDON HU12 40 B4
Belmont St HULLE HU9 37 F1
Belprin Rd BEV HU17 5 G4
Belton Cl SINGS HU8 26 B1
Belvedere Dr SPR/BIL HU11 16 D5
Belvedere Rd HESSLE HU13 49 F2
Belvoir St SUL/NEW HU5 35 F1
Bempton Gv SUL/NEW HU5 34 B1
Benedict Cl ANLPK/PPK HU4 49 G2
Benedict Rd ANLPK/PPK HU4 49 G2
Bennington Cl HEDON HU12 41 F4
Bentley Ct CHULLW HU3 35 E4
Bentley Gv HULLN HU6 22 D2
Berberis Cl CHULLW HU3 35 G4
Beresford Av HULLE HU9 * 37 F1
HULLN HU6 23 H2
Beretun Gn BTNUH DN18 52 D4
Bergen Wy BRAN HU7 13 H5
Berkeley Dr BEV HU17 6 D3
HEDON HU12 41 E4
Berkeley St CHULLW HU3 23 H5
Berkshire Cl BEV HU17 6 D4
Berkshire St SINGS HU8 25 E5
Bermondsey Dr SUL/NEW HU5 34 C1
Bernadette Av ANLPK/PPK HU4 33 H4
Berryman Wy HESSLE HU13 49 G1
Bessacarr Av ANL/KKEL HU10 21 F5
Bessingby Gv HULLE HU9 26 B4
Beta Vls CHULLW HU3 * 35 G1
Bethell Ct HEDON HU12 41 F3
Bethnal Gn HULLN HU6 * 23 H2
Bethune Av ANLPK/PPK HU4 49 G1
Bethune Av West HESSLE HU13 49 G2
Beverley 20 BEV HU17 6 A2
BR/NC/SC HU15 45 E1
COT/SKID HU16 10 A3
Beverley Dr BEV HU17 4 C2
Beverley Parklands BEV HU17 7 F2
Beverley Parks Crossing
BEV HU17 7 G5
Beverley Rd ANL/KKEL HU10 20 C5
ANL/KKEL HU10 32 D1
BR/NC/SC HU15 43 E2
CHULLW HU3 35 H1
COT/SKID HU16 10 C3
HESSLE HU13 33 E5
HULLN HU6 23 G1
SUL/NEW HU5 23 H3
Bewholme Gv HULLE HU9 38 B1
Bewick Gv HULLE HU9 25 H4
Bexhill Av HULLE HU9 27 E4
Bibury Cl SINGS HU8 24 D4
Bickerton Cl HULLN HU6 12 D4
Bickleigh Gv SINGS HU8 * 16 C5
Bideford Gv HULLE HU9 27 E5
Bielby Dr BEV HU17 7 G1
Biggin Av BRAN HU7 15 E3
Bilsdale Gv HULLE HU9 37 H1
Bilton Gv HULLE HU9 26 B4
Bilton Rd SPR/BIL HU11 17 E5
Binbrook Garth BRAN HU7 14 D1
Binfield Sq SUL/NEW HU5 * 23 G4
Birch Cl BEV HU17 5 E3
BR/NC/SC HU15 * 44 D5
HESSLE HU13 48 B1
SUL/NEW HU5 33 H2
Birch Cft BR/NC/SC HU15 44 C3
Birchdale BTNUH DN18 52 D5
Birch Dr ANL/KKEL HU10 21 E5
Birch Gdns BTNUH DN18 52 D3
Birch Leigh CHULLW HU3 35 G3
Birch Tree Dr HEDON HU12 40 C4
Birchwood Av SUL/NEW HU5 33 G2
Birch Wood Cl BTNUH DN18 52 C3
Birdforth Ms SUL/NEW HU5 22 B3
Birdsall Av SUL/NEW HU5 22 A4
Birdsall Cl COT/SKID HU16 21 E1
Birkdale Cl ANL/KKEL HU10 32 B1
Birkdale Wy HULLE HU9 37 F1
Birklands Dr SINGS HU8 25 G2
Bishop Alcock Rd
SUL/NEW HU5 22 B3
Bishop Blunt Cl HESSLE HU13 49 F3
Bishopcockin Cl HESSLE HU13 49 G3
Bishop Gurdon Cl HESSLE HU13 49 F3
Bishop Kempthorne Clo
HESSLE HU13 49 F3
Bishop La CHULLS HU1 2 E4
Bishop Lane Staith CHULLS HU1 2 E4
Bishops Cft BEV HU17 6 D1
Bishop Temple Ct HESSLE HU13 49 F1
Bisley Gv BRAN HU7 14 C4
Bittern Cl ANLPK/PPK HU4 50 B2
BTNUH DN18 52 C2
Blackburn Av BR/NC/SC HU15 44 C4
Blackfriargate CHULLS HU1 2 E5
Blackhall Cl BRAN HU7 9 E5
Blackhope Cl BRAN HU7 9 G5
Blacksmiths Cl BRWUH DN19 54 D4
Blackthorn Cl CHULLW HU3 35 H3
Blackthorn La ANL/KKEL HU10 33 F2
Blackwater Wy BRAN HU7 9 E5
Bladons Wk ANL/KKEL HU10 32 D1
Blaides Staithe CHULLS HU1 3 F3
Blake Cl CHULLN HU2 36 A1
Blandford Cl BRAN HU7 14 D5
Blanket Rw CHULLS HU1 2 D5
Blaycourt HULLN HU6 12 C5
Blaydes St HULLN HU6 23 H2
Bleach Yd BEV HU17 * 4 C4
Blenheim Rd BEV HU17 6 D3
Blenheim St SUL/NEW HU5 35 F1
Blenkin St HULLE HU9 3 G1
Blisland Cl BRAN HU7 14 B2
Bloomfield Av SUL/NEW HU5 34 A1
Bloomsbury Ct CHULLW HU3 35 H3
Blossom Gv SINGS HU8 15 F3
Blucher La BEV HU17 7 F1
Blueberry Ct ANLPK/PPK HU4 34 A5
Blundell Cl CHULLN HU2 36 A1
Blyth Ct BTNUH DN18 53 F5
Blythorpe HULLN HU6 12 D3
Blyth St HULLE HU9 3 G1
Boatswain Cft CHULLS HU1 2 C6
Bobbers Staith CHULLW HU3 35 H5
Bodmin Rd BRAN HU7 14 B3
Boggle La SPR/BIL HU11 19 E2
Boldron Ms SUL/NEW HU5 22 B3
Boltby Ms SUL/NEW HU5 22 C3
Bon Accord Rd HESSLE HU13 49 E3
Bondane HULLN HU6 12 C4
Bond St CHULLS HU1 2 C2
HEDON HU12 41 F4
Bondyke Cl COT/SKID HU16 11 E5
Bonfrey Wy HEDON HU12 * 41 F4
Bontoft Av SUL/NEW HU5 22 C5
Boothferry Rd ANLPK/PPK HU4 34 C4
HESSLE HU13 48 B3
Borella Gv CHULLW HU3 35 E5
Borodales HEDON HU12 40 C4
Borrowdale BRAN HU7 14 B5
Borthwick Cl BRAN HU7 9 G4
Borwick Dr BEV HU17 5 H5
Bossington Cl BRAN HU7 14 C2
Boston Ct BRAN HU7 14 A1
Bothwell Gv HULLE HU9 38 D1
Boulevard CHULLW HU3 35 F4
Boulsworth Av HULLN HU6 13 G4
Boulton Gv HULLE HU9 25 G4
Bournemouth St
SUL/NEW HU5 24 A4
Bourne St CHULLN HU2 2 D2
Bowlalley La CHULLS HU1 2 D4
Bowmandale BTNUH DN18 52 D5
Bowmont Wy BRAN HU7 9 E5
Bow Rd BR/NC/SC HU15 45 H2
Boxtree Wk CHULLW HU3 * 35 G4
Boynton St CHULLW HU3 35 G5
B P Av CHULLW HU3 * 34 D4
Brackendale Cl BRAN HU7 24 D2
Brackley Cl SINGS HU8 24 D4
Braddon Gv BEV HU17 * 7 G5
Bradford Av HULLE HU9 27 E4
Bradgate Pk BRAN HU7 14 A1
Bradwell Cl BTNUH DN18 52 C4
Braemar Av HULLN HU6 13 F5
Braid Hill Dr BRAN HU7 15 F2
Braids Wk ANL/KKEL HU10 32 B1
Bramble Garth BEV HU17 5 E2
Bramble Hl BEV HU17 6 D3
The Brambles BRWUH DN19 54 D4
Brandesburton St CHULLW HU3 35 F1
Brandon Ct SINGS HU8 25 E5
Brandon Wy BRAN HU7 9 F5
Brandsby Gv HULLE HU9 26 D3
Bransdale Gv HULLE HU9 37 H1
Bransholme Rd BRAN HU7 15 E1
Brantingham Cl
COT/SKID HU16 11 E5
Brantingham Wk
SUL/NEW HU5 22 A5
Brazil St HULLE HU9 37 E1
Bream Ct HULLN HU6 13 F3
Brecon Av SINGS HU8 * 25 E5
Brecon Dr BRAN HU7 9 F5
Brecon St SINGS HU8 25 E5
Brendon Av SINGS HU8 24 D3
Brent Av SINGS HU8 16 B5
Brentwood Av HULLE HU9 * 37 E1
SUL/NEW HU5 * 35 F1
Brentwood Cl BR/NC/SC HU15 44 B4
Brentwood Vls CHULLW HU3 * 35 E3
SUL/NEW HU5 * 23 G4
Brereton Cl BEV HU17 4 D3
Bretherdale BRAN HU7 14 B5
Brevere Rd HEDON HU12 41 F3
Briarfield Rd SUL/NEW HU5 22 D4
The Briars HESSLE HU13 49 E1
Briarwood Cl BRAN HU7 15 E2
Bricknell Av SUL/NEW HU5 22 C3
Brickyard La NF/SW HU14 46 A4
Bridge Cl HULLE HU9 3 K3
Bridgegate Dr HULLE HU9 3 K3
Bridge Rd BR/NC/SC HU15 42 B3
The Bridges BTNUH DN18 53 E5
Bridlington Av CHULLN HU2 36 B1
Bridport Cl BRAN HU7 15 E4
Brigg Dr HESSLE HU13 49 F1
Brigham Gv HULLE HU9 26 B5
Brighton St CHULLW HU3 51 E1
Bright St SINGS HU8 36 D1
Brimham Ms SINGS HU8 * 15 G5
Brimington Rd ANL/KKEL HU10 21 F4
Brimley BEV HU17 4 B4
Brimley Gn BEV HU17 4 B4
Brindley St HULLE HU9 25 G4
Brisbane St CHULLW HU3 35 H4
Bristol Rd SUL/NEW HU5 34 A1
Britannia Gdns SUL/NEW HU5 24 A5
Brixham Ct CHULLW HU3 35 E4
Brixton Cl SINGS HU8 25 G1
Broadacre Pk BR/NC/SC HU15 45 E3
Broadland Dr HULLE HU9 26 A2
Broad Lane Cl COT/SKID HU16 11 H4
Broadley Av ANL/KKEL HU10 32 D3
Broadley Cl HULLE HU9 3 J1
Broadley Cft BR/NC/SC HU15 45 E4
Broadley Wy BR/NC/SC HU15 45 E4
Broad Oak SPR/BIL HU11 16 D5
Broadstairs Cl SINGS HU8 15 G4
Broadstone Cl BRAN HU7 15 E5
Broadwaters BRAN HU7 13 H1
Broadway Dr HULLE HU9 26 A3
The Broadway HULLE HU9 26 A3
Brockenhurst Av
COT/SKID HU16 12 B5
Brockle Bank Ct HEDON HU12 28 D5
Brocklesby Cl HESSLE HU13 49 G1
Brockley Cl SINGS HU8 15 G5
Brockton Cl CHULLW HU3 34 C4
Brodsworth St SINGS HU8 37 E1
Bromley St CHULLN HU2 36 B1
Brompton Cl ANL/KKEL HU10 33 G3
SUL/NEW HU5 22 C4
Brompton Ct CHULLW HU3 23 H5
Bromwich Rd ANL/KKEL HU10 33 F1
Brookfield Cl BRAN HU7 14 A2
Brookholme BEV HU17 7 G2
Brooklands BRAN HU7 25 E1
Brooklands Cl BEV HU17 5 F3
Brooklands Pk COT/SKID HU16 11 G5
Brooklands Rd SUL/NEW HU5 34 C1
Brooklyn Av SUL/NEW HU5 * 23 H3
Brooklyn St SUL/NEW HU5 23 H3
Brooklyn Ter SUL/NEW HU5 * 23 H3
Brooklyn Vls HULLE HU9 * 38 C2
Brookside BR/NC/SC HU15 45 F3
Brook St CHULLN HU2 2 B3
Broomhead Cl SINGS HU8 15 G4
Brougham St CHULLW HU3 34 D2
Brough Rd BR/NC/SC HU15 42 D3
Browning Cl CHULLW HU3 35 H1
Brucella Gv CHULLW HU3 35 E5
Brumby's Ter HULLE HU9 37 F2
Brunslow Cl CHULLW HU3 34 C4
Brunswick Av CHULLN HU2 36 A1
CHULLW HU3 36 A1
HULLE HU9 * 3 J1
Brunswick Gv HESSLE HU13 49 E2
Brunswick Ter SINGS HU8 * 25 E5
Buccaneer Wy BR/NC/SC HU15 44 C5
Buckingham St SINGS HU8 25 E5
Buckland Cl SINGS HU8 16 C4
Bude Rd BRAN HU7 14 A1
Budworth Pk BRAN HU7 13 H1
Bullers Ct CHULLW HU3 * 35 E4
Bull Pasture BR/NC/SC HU15 42 C4
Burbage Av SINGS HU8 25 E2
Burcott Garth ANLPK/PPK HU4 49 H1
Burdale Cl HULLE HU9 26 B3
HULLE HU9 26 B4
Burden Cl BEV HU17 5 F4
Burden Rd BEV HU17 5 F3
Burden St CHULLS HU1 2 B3
Burdon Cl ANL/KKEL HU10 33 F2
Burgate BTNUH DN18 53 E3
Burgess Sq HEDON HU12 41 E3
Burleigh St SINGS HU8 37 E1
Burlington Rd SINGS HU8 25 F2
Burma Dr HULLE HU9 38 B1
Burnaby Cl BEV HU17 4 D3
Burnby Cl SUL/NEW HU5 22 A4
Burney Cl BEV HU17 4 D4
Burnham Rd ANLPK/PPK HU4 49 H1
Burniston Rd SUL/NEW HU5 22 C4
Burnsalls Rd HEDON HU12 40 C3
Burrill La BR/NC/SC HU15 43 G5
Burrill Ms SUL/NEW HU5 22 C3
The Burrs BR/NC/SC HU15 44 B4
Burslem St CHULLN HU2 36 A1
Burton Rd BEV HU17 4 B3
COT/SKID HU16 21 F1
Bush Cl ANLPK/PPK HU4 50 B1
Bushey Pk BRAN HU7 13 H1
Butcher Rw BEV HU17 4 D5
Butchers Rw BRAN HU7 * 15 F5
Butforth La BRWUH DN19 55 G3
Buttercup Cl HULLE HU9 37 F2
Butterfly Mdw BEV HU17 4 A4
Buttermere Cl ANLPK/PPK HU4 34 C3
Buttfield Rd HESSLE HU13 49 E3
Butt La BEV HU17 6 D2
Butts Rd BTNUH DN18 53 E3
Buxton Vls HULLE HU9 * 37 F1
Byland Ct HULLE HU9 37 G1
Byron St SINGS HU8 25 F4

C

Cadeleigh Cl BRAN HU7 14 C3
Cadogan Av CHULLW HU3 * 35 F4
Cadogan Gv CHULLW HU3 * 35 F4
Cadogan St CHULLW HU3 35 F4
Caistor Rd BTNUH DN18 53 E4
Caldane HULLN HU6 12 C3

Caldberg Ms *SUL/NEW* HU5 22 C3
Calderdale *BRAN* HU7 14 B5
Calder Gv *SINGS* HU8 16 C5
Calder Sq *BR/NC/SC* HU15 * 45 E4
Caledon Cl *HULLE* HU9 26 D1
Caledonia Pk *HULLE* HU9 3 H5
Callow Hill Dr *BRAN* HU7 15 F2
Calthorpe Gdns *CHULLW* HU3 * 34 D5
Calthorpe St *CHULLW* HU3 35 F4
Calthwaite Dr *BR/NC/SC* HU15 45 E5
Calvert La *ANLPK/PPK* HU4 34 B2
Calvert Rd *SUL/NEW* HU5 34 B1
Cambeak Cl *BRAN* HU7 14 B1
Camberwell Wy *SINGS* HU8 26 A1
Camborne Gv *SINGS* HU8 24 D3
Cambrian Av *HULLE* HU9 * 37 F1
Cambridge Gv *HULLE* HU9 25 H5
Cambridge Rd *HESSLE* HU13 49 E1
Cambridge St *CHULLW* HU3 35 H3
Camden St *CHULLW* HU3 35 F4
Camelford Cl *BRAN* HU7 14 B2
Camerton Gv *HULLE* HU9 25 H4
Cam Gv *SINGS* HU8 16 C5
Camilla Cl *HULLE* HU9 3 F5
Campbell Ct *HULLE* HU9 26 A4
Campbell St *CHULLW* HU3 35 H4
Camperdown *SPR/BIL* HU11 16 D5
Campion Av *ANLPK/PPK* HU4 49 H2
Canada Dr *COT/SKID* HU16 21 E1
Canberra St *CHULLW* HU3 35 H4
Cannon St *CHULLN* HU2 36 B1
Canongate *COT/SKID* HU16 11 H4
Canon Tardrew Cl
HESSLE HU13 49 F3
Canopias Cl *CHULLW* HU3 35 E5
Canterbury Cl *BEV* HU17 6 C3
Canterbury Dr *SINGS* HU8 15 G3
Capstan Rd *HULLN* HU6 13 G3
Captains Wk *CHULLS* HU1 2 B6
Carden Av *HULLE* HU9 26 C4
Cardigan Av *CHULLW* HU3 * 34 D2
SUL/NEW HU5 * 24 A5
Cardigan Rd *CHULLW* HU3 34 C2
Carew St *CHULLW* HU3 34 D2
Carholme Vls *HULLE* HU9 * 25 F5
Carisbrooke Av *CHULLW* HU3 * 34 D2
COT/SKID HU16 11 H5
SINGS HU8 * 24 D5
SUL/NEW HU5 * 23 G3
Carisbrooke Vls
SUL/NEW HU5 * 23 F4
Carlam La *BRAN* HU7 9 F3
Carlisle Av *CHULLW* HU3 * 35 F4
Carlton Av *HULLE* HU9 * 38 B2
SUL/NEW HU5 * 23 F4
Carlton Ct *BEV* HU17 4 D5
Carlton Ri *BEV* HU17 6 D4
Carlton Rd *BR/NC/SC* HU15 44 D3
Carlton St *CHULLW* HU3 35 E5
Carlton Ter *SINGS* HU8 * 25 E5
Carlton Vls *CHULLW* HU3 * 35 E4
SUL/NEW HU5 * 23 G4
Carnaby Gv *HULLN* HU6 22 C1
Carnegie St *CHULLW* HU3 35 E3
Carnoustie Cl *SINGS* HU8 25 E3
Carol Dickson Ct *CHULLW* HU3 35 G4
Caroline Pl *CHULLN* HU2 2 C1
Carolines Pl *COT/SKID* HU16 10 B3
Caroline St *CHULLN* HU2 36 B1
Carperby Ms *SUL/NEW* HU5 22 B3
Carr Cl *BEV* HU17 5 F5
Carrington Av *CHULLW* HU3 * 34 D2
COT/SKID HU16 11 H5
SUL/NEW HU5 * 23 G3
Carrington St *CHULLW* HU3 35 F4
Carr La *ANL/KKEL* HU10 20 D5
CHULLS HU1 2 B4
Carroll Pl *CHULLS* HU1 2 E2
Carr Rd *BEV* HU17 4 D1
Carr St *CHULLN* HU2 36 B1
Carter Dr *BEV* HU17 4 D2
Cartmel Ct *HULLE* HU9 26 B4
Cartwright La *BEV* HU17 6 C2
Castle Ct *BTNUH* DN18 53 E4
Castle Dr *BR/NC/SC* HU15 42 C2
Castledyke South
BTNUH DN18 53 E4
Castledyke West *BTNUH* DN18 52 D3
Castleford Gv *HULLE* HU9 27 E5
Castle Gn *COT/SKID* HU16 11 E5
Castle Gv *SUL/NEW* HU5 * 35 E1
Castle Hall Rd *BRAN* HU7 * 14 D2
Castlehill Rd *BRAN* HU7 15 F3
Castle Ri *BR/NC/SC* HU15 42 C2
Castle Rd *COT/SKID* HU16 20 D1
Castle St *CHULLS* HU1 2 C5
Castleton Av *SUL/NEW* HU5 22 C3
Castle Wy *HESSLE* HU13 49 E4
Catford Cl *SINGS* HU8 25 G1
Cathedral Cl *BEV* HU17 6 D3
Catherine Gv *CHULLW* HU3 * 35 F4
Catherine McAuley Cl
HULLN HU6 23 G2
Catherine St *BTNUH* DN18 53 E3
CHULLN HU2 * 36 B1
Catterick Ms *SUL/NEW* HU5 * 22 B3
Caughey St *CHULLN* HU2 35 H2
The Causeway *BEV* HU17 5 E5
Cave Crs *COT/SKID* HU16 11 E5
Cavendish Dr *BEV* HU17 6 D3
Cavendish Pk *BR/NC/SC* HU15 44 C4
Cavendish Rd *SINGS* HU8 25 F1
Cavendish Sq *CHULLW* HU3 23 H5
Cave Rd *BR/NC/SC* HU15 44 A2
Cave St *SUL/NEW* HU5 23 H5
Cavill Pl *CHULLW* HU3 35 H4
Cawood Av *HULLE* HU9 * 3 J1
Cawthorne Dr *ANLPK/PPK* HU4 50 A1
Cayley Rd *ANL/KKEL* HU10 33 F3
Cayton Rd *SINGS* HU8 25 F2
Cecil St *CHULLW* HU3 34 D4
Cedar Av *COT/SKID* HU16 11 G5
Cedar Cl *ANL/KKEL* HU10 32 D3
BRAN HU7 9 E2
Cedar Ct *HEDON* HU12 40 C3
Cedar Gv *CHULLW* HU3 * 34 D4
HULLE HU9 * 37 F1
The Cedar Gv *BEV* HU17 4 B3
The Cedars *SUL/NEW* HU5 * 23 G3
Cedarwood Dr *SUL/NEW* HU5 33 H2
Celandine Cl *SUL/NEW* HU5 22 B5
Central Av *BEV* HU17 6 C1
Central St *CHULLN* HU2 24 B5
Centurion Wy *BR/NC/SC* HU15 44 C4
Century Rd *HEDON* HU12 39 G2
Ceylon St *HULLE* HU9 38 B2
Chadcourt *HULLN* HU6 12 C5
Chalfont Cl *HESSLE* HU13 48 D2
Chamberlain Cl *BRAN* HU7 15 F5
Chamberlain Ct *BRAN* HU7 15 F5
Chamberlain Gdns *SINGS* HU8 25 E3
Chamberlain Rd *SINGS* HU8 24 D3
Chamberlain St *BRAN* HU7 15 F5
Champney Rd *BEV* HU17 6 D1
Champneys Cl *HESSLE* HU13 49 E3
Chancery Ct *SUL/NEW* HU5 34 C1
Chancewaters *BRAN* HU7 13 H1
Chandlers Ct *HULLE* HU9 3 J3
Chanterlands Av
SUL/NEW HU5 35 E1
Chantreys Dr *BR/NC/SC* HU15 44 C3
Chantry La *BEV* HU17 7 E1
Chantry Wy *NF/SW* HU14 31 E4
Chantry Wy East *NF/SW* HU14 31 E4
Chapel Cl *BRWUH* DN19 55 E5
COT/SKID HU16 10 A3
HEDON HU12 28 D5
HESSLE HU13 49 G3
Chapel Hl *BR/NC/SC* HU15 45 G3
Chapel La *ANL/KKEL* HU10 31 H2
BRAN HU7 8 D2
BTNUH DN18 52 D3
CHULLS HU1 2 E3
Chapel Lane Staith *CHULLS* HU1 2 E3
Chapel Ms *BR/NC/SC* HU15 44 C2
Chapelry Garth *HEDON* HU12 41 E3
Chapel St *CHULLS* HU1 2 B3
Chapman St *SINGS* HU8 36 D1
Charing Cl *SUL/NEW* HU5 35 G1
Chariot St *CHULLS* HU1 2 B4
Charles Brady Ct *HULLE* HU9 * 26 C1
Charles M Jacobs Homes
ANLPK/PPK HU4 * 34 B5
Charles St *CHULLN* HU2 2 B1
HEDON HU12 41 E4
Charlestown Wy *HULLE* HU9 3 K3
Charlotte St *CHULLS* HU1 2 E2
Charlotte Street Ms
CHULLS HU1 2 D2
Charlton Vls *HULLE* HU9 * 37 G1
Charnock Av *SINGS* HU8 26 A2
Charnwood Cl *BRAN* HU7 9 E5
Charterfield *SPR/BIL* HU11 16 D5
Charterhouse La *CHULLN* HU2 2 D1
Chatham Av *SUL/NEW* HU5 * 23 G3
Chatham St *CHULLW* HU3 34 D2
Chatsworth Av *SUL/NEW* HU5 * 35 F1
Chatsworth Cl *BEV* HU17 6 D2
Chatsworth St *SUL/NEW* HU5 35 F1
Chaucer St *SINGS* HU8 25 E4
Chaytor Cl *HEDON* HU12 41 E4
Cheadle Cl *CHULLN* HU2 36 A1
Chelmer Rd *SINGS* HU8 26 B1
Chelmsford Cl *HULLE* HU9 27 E5
Chelsea Cl *SINGS* HU8 25 H1
Chelsea Ct *COT/SKID* HU16 21 F1
Cheltenham Av *BRAN* HU7 14 C4
Cheriton Cl *BRAN* HU7 14 B2
Cherry Garth *BEV* HU17 5 F5
CHULLW HU3 35 E4
Cherry La *BRWUH* DN19 55 E3
SINGS HU8 25 E2
Cherry Tree Av *SINGS* HU8 25 E4
Cherry Tree Cl *SPR/BIL* HU11 17 G5
Cherry Tree Crossing *BEV* HU17 5 E5
Cherry Tree La *BEV* HU17 5 E5
HEDON HU12 41 E3
Cherry Trees *COT/SKID* HU16 10 A3
Cherry Tree Ter *BEV* HU17 5 F5
Cheshire Cl *SUL/NEW* HU5 22 B5
Chesnut Av *SUL/NEW* HU5 23 G4
Chester Av *BEV* HU17 6 D4
SUL/NEW HU5 * 24 A5
Chester Gv *CHULLW* HU3 * 35 F4
Chesterholme *SPR/BIL* HU11 16 D5
Chester Rd *SUL/NEW* HU5 21 H5
Chestnut Av *ANL/KKEL* HU10 33 E1
BEV HU17 5 E3
CHULLW HU3 * 34 D4
HEDON HU12 40 D2
HESSLE HU13 49 E3
SINGS HU8 * 24 D5
Chestnut Cl *BEV* HU17 5 E3
Chestnut Gv *SINGS* HU8 24 D4
SPR/BIL HU11 19 E1
Chestnut Ri *BRWUH* DN19 54 D4
The Chestnuts *SUL/NEW* HU5 * 23 F4
Chevening Pk *BRAN* HU7 13 H1
Cheviotdale *BRAN* HU7 14 B5
Chevy Cha *SPR/BIL* HU11 17 E5
The Chilterns *HULLE* HU9 26 D4
Chilton Ri *ANL/KKEL* HU10 20 B5
Chilton St *CHULLW* HU3 35 F4
Chiswick Cl *SINGS* HU8 26 A1
Cholmley St *CHULLW* HU3 35 F4
Church Av *NF/SW* HU14 46 D4
Church Cl *ANL/KKEL* HU10 33 E3
BRAN HU7 15 F5
Church Crs *BRAN* HU7 8 D2
Church Fld *HESSLE* HU13 49 F1
Church Ga *HEDON* HU12 40 D3
Church Gn *BEV* HU17 4 A3
Church Hl *BR/NC/SC* HU15 42 C2
Churchill Av *CHULLW* HU3 * 34 D2
COT/SKID HU16 11 F5
Churchill Gv *SUL/NEW* HU5 * 23 H3
Churchill Vls *HULLE* HU9 * 37 F1
Church La *ANL/KKEL* HU10 32 C1
BR/NC/SC HU15 44 C1
BRAN HU7 9 E2
HEDON HU12 40 D3
HULLE HU9 38 C1
SPR/BIL HU11 17 E5
SPR/BIL HU11 19 E2
Church Lane Staith
CHULLS HU1 2 E4
Church Ms *NF/SW* HU14 * 31 G4
Church Ri *COT/SKID* HU16 10 A3
Church Rd *BEV* HU17 4 A3
BRAN HU7 8 D2
NF/SW HU14 46 D4
Church Rw *SINGS* HU8 36 C1
Churchside *BRWUH* DN19 55 E4
Church St *ANL/KKEL* HU10 33 E3
BR/NC/SC HU15 42 C3
BR/NC/SC HU15 44 C1
BRAN HU7 15 F4
HULLE HU9 3 G2
SINGS HU8 15 G5
Church Vw *BEV* HU17 5 F5
BR/NC/SC HU15 44 C1
BTNUH DN18 53 E4
Church Wy *SUL/NEW* HU5 34 C2
The Circle *HESSLE* HU13 48 D2
Citadel Ct *BEV* HU17 5 E5
Citadel Wy *HULLE* HU9 3 G4
Cladshaw *HULLN* HU6 12 D3
Clairbrook Cl *CHULLW* HU3 35 E4
Clanthorpe *HULLN* HU6 12 D3
Clapham Av *SINGS* HU8 25 G1
Clapson's La *BTNUH* DN18 52 D2
Clare Ct *BEV* HU17 5 G5
Clare Gv *HULLE* HU9 26 A5
Claremont Av *HULLN* HU6 23 H2
SUL/NEW HU5 * 35 F1
Clarence Av *HULLE* HU9 * 38 B1
SINGS HU8 25 G2
Clarence Ct *CHULLN* HU2 2 C2
Clarence St *HULLE* HU9 3 G2
Clarendon Av *SUL/NEW* HU5 * 23 G3
Clarendon St *CHULLW* HU3 35 H2
Clarondale *BRAN* HU7 14 A4
Clay St *SINGS* HU8 24 C3
Clear View Cl *SINGS* HU8 15 H5
Clearwaters *BRAN* HU7 13 H1
Cleaves Av *BR/NC/SC* HU15 43 E2
Cleeve Dr *BRAN* HU7 14 C2
Cleeve Rd *HEDON* HU12 41 F5
Cleveland St *SINGS* HU8 24 C5
Cliff Gv *BTNUH* DN18 52 D4
Cliff House Dr *HESSLE* HU13 48 C4
Clifford Av *SINGS* HU8 25 G2
Cliff Rd *HESSLE* HU13 48 C5
Cliff Top La *HESSLE* HU13 48 C4
Clifton Gdns *CHULLW* HU3 * 35 E4
SUL/NEW HU5 * 23 F4
Clifton St *CHULLN* HU2 36 A1
Clifton Ter *SUL/NEW* HU5 24 A5
Clinton Av *SUL/NEW* HU5 * 23 G3
Clivedale Av *SUL/NEW* HU5 * 23 G3
Clive Sullivan Wy *HESSLE* HU13 48 A4
Clive V *HULLE* HU9 * 37 G1
Cloeberry Wy *HEDON* HU12 40 C4
The Cloisters *BEV* HU17 * 7 E1
The Close *ANL/KKEL* HU10 21 F5
BRAN HU7 15 F5
COT/SKID HU16 21 F1
Clough Garth *HEDON* HU12 41 E3
Clough Rd *HULLN* HU6 24 A3
Cloughton Gv *SUL/NEW* HU5 22 C4
Clovelly Av *CHULLW* HU3 * 34 D2
SUL/NEW HU5 * 23 G3
Clovelly Gdns *SUL/NEW* HU5 24 A4
Clover Bank Vw *HULLN* HU6 13 G2
Clowes Ct *HESSLE* HU13 49 E3
Clumber St *SUL/NEW* HU5 35 F1
Clydesdale Av *CHULLW* HU3 * 34 D4
Clyde St *CHULLW* HU3 34 D4
The Coachings *HESSLE* HU13 48 D5
Cobden St *CHULLW* HU3 34 D2
Cock Pit Cl *ANL/KKEL* HU10 32 C3
Coelus St *HULLE* HU9 3 F2
Cogan St *CHULLS* HU1 2 A5
CHULLW HU3 * 35 H3
Cohort Cl *BR/NC/SC* HU15 44 C4
Coldstream Cl *SINGS* HU8 26 C1
Coleford Gv *BRAN* HU7 14 C4
Colemans Rd *HEDON* HU12 40 C4
Colenso Av *HULLE* HU9 * 37 F1
Colenso St *CHULLW* HU3 35 E4
Colenso Vls *SINGS* HU8 * 24 D5
Coleridge St *SINGS* HU8 25 F4
College Gv *HULLE* HU9 25 H5
College Rd *BRWUH* DN19 55 F4
College St *BRAN* HU7 15 F5
CHULLW HU3 2 A1
Colleridge Gv *BEV* HU17 6 B4
Collier Cl *NF/SW* HU14 46 C4
Collier St *CHULLS* HU1 2 A3
Collin Av *HULLE* HU9 26 C4
Collingwood St *CHULLW* HU3 35 H2
Collynson Cl *ANL/KKEL* HU10 33 E1
Colonial St *CHULLN* HU2 35 H2
Coltman Av *BEV* HU17 5 E4
Coltman Cl *BEV* HU17 5 E2
Coltman St *CHULLW* HU3 35 G4
Colville Av *ANLPK/PPK* HU4 33 H3
Colwall Av *SUL/NEW* HU5 22 B4
Colwyn Cl *BRAN* HU7 9 G4
Commerce La *CHULLW* HU3 35 H4
Commercial Rd *CHULLS* HU1 2 B5
Commodore Cft *CHULLS* HU1 2 C6
Common La *BR/NC/SC* HU15 45 F5
BRAN HU7 9 E2
Common Lane Br *BRAN* HU7 9 H1
Common Rd *BR/NC/SC* HU15 42 B4
Compass Rd *HULLN* HU6 13 G3
Conduit St *CHULLS* HU1 3 F4
Conifer Cl *SUL/NEW* HU5 34 A2
Conington Av *BEV* HU17 5 G5
Conisborough Ms
BR/NC/SC HU15 45 E5
Coniston Gv *HULLE* HU9 25 H4
Coniston La *SPR/BIL* HU11 17 H1
Connaught Rd *BRAN* HU7 13 G2
Consort Ct *HULLE* HU9 3 G5
Constable Av *SPR/BIL* HU11 17 F4
Constable Cl *SPR/BIL* HU11 19 E1
Constable Garth *HEDON* HU12 41 F3
Constable St *CHULLW* HU3 35 G5
Constable Wy *BR/NC/SC* HU15 45 E5
Constantine Cl *BRAN* HU7 14 C2
Convent La *CHULLW* HU3 35 H3
Conway Cl *CHULLW* HU3 35 F4
Cookbury Cl *BRAN* HU7 14 A2
Coombs Yd *BEV* HU17 4 D4
Cooper St *BEV* HU17 5 E4
CHULLN HU2 36 B1
Copandale Rd *BEV* HU17 4 C4
Copenhagen Rd *BRAN* HU7 24 B1
Copper Beech Cl *NF/SW* HU14 47 E1
Coppice Side *ANLPK/PPK* HU4 34 A3
The Copse *BEV* HU17 7 G1
Corbridge Cl *HULLE* HU9 27 E5
Corby Pk *NF/SW* HU14 46 C3
Cordella Cl *CHULLW* HU3 35 E4
Coriander Cl *BEV* HU17 6 D2
Corinthian Wy *HULLE* HU9 37 F3
Cormorant Cl *BRAN* HU7 15 F3
Cornhill Cots *BTNUH* DN18 * 53 H4
Cornhill Dr *BTNUH* DN18 53 G4
Cornwall Gdns *CHULLW* HU3 * 35 G4
SUL/NEW HU5 * 23 G3
Cornwall St *COT/SKID* HU16 12 A5
SINGS HU8 24 C5
Corona Dr *SINGS* HU8 25 E2
Coronation Av *HULLE* HU9 * 25 F5
Coronation Cl *BEV* HU17 5 F4
Coronation Rd North
SUL/NEW HU5 22 A5
Coronation Rd South
SUL/NEW HU5 21 H5
Coronet Cl *HULLN* HU6 13 F3
Corporation Rd *BEV* HU17 4 D5
HULLE HU9 38 B3
Corran Garth *ANLPK/PPK* HU4 49 G1
Corsair Gv *CHULLW* HU3 35 E5
Cosford Garth *BRAN* HU7 14 D1
The Cotswolds *HULLE* HU9 26 D4
Cottage Dr *ANL/KKEL* HU10 32 B2
Cottage Gn *COT/SKID* HU16 21 G1
Cottage La *BTNUH* DN18 53 E4
Cottage Ms *BEV* HU17 5 E5
Cotterdale *BRAN* HU7 14 A4
Cottesmore Rd *HESSLE* HU13 49 F2
Cottingham Av *CHULLS* HU1 * 2 A4
Cottingham Gv *HULLN* HU6 22 D2
Cottingham Rd *HULLN* HU6 22 D2
SUL/NEW HU5 22 C2
Coulson Dr *HESSLE* HU13 49 F2
Coultas Ct *CHULLW* HU3 35 E3
Council Av *ANLPK/PPK* HU4 50 B1
Council Ter *BTNUH* DN18 52 D3
Countess Cl *HULLN* HU6 13 F3
County Rd North
SUL/NEW HU5 22 B5
County Rd South
SUL/NEW HU5 34 A1
Coupland Gdns *SUL/NEW* HU5 24 A4
Courtland Rd *HULLN* HU6 12 C4
Courtney St *SINGS* HU8 36 D1
Courtpark Rd *HULLN* HU6 12 D4
Courtway Rd *HULLN* HU6 12 C4
Coventry Rd *SUL/NEW* HU5 22 A5
Coverdale *BRAN* HU7 14 B4
The Covert *COT/SKID* HU16 22 A1
Covington *BR/NC/SC* HU15 44 D3
Cowden Gv *HULLE* HU9 26 A4
Cowgate *BR/NC/SC* HU15 45 F3
Coxwold Gv *ANLPK/PPK* HU4 34 C4
Cradley Rd *SUL/NEW* HU5 22 A3
Cranberry Wy *ANLPK/PPK* HU4 34 A5
Cranbourne Av
SUL/NEW HU5 * 24 A4
Cranbourne St *CHULLW* HU3 35 G1
Cranbrook Av *HULLN* HU6 23 F2
Crane Rd *HULLE* HU9 3 J4
Cranham Gv *BRAN* HU7 14 C4
Cranswick Gv *HULLE* HU9 26 B5
Crathorne Rd *BEV* HU17 5 F4
Craven Ct *HULLE* HU9 3 K1
Craven St North *HULLE* HU9 37 E1
Craven St South *HULLE* HU9 37 F2
Crawshaw Av *BEV* HU17 4 D3
Crayford Cl *HULLE* HU9 27 F5
Crescent St *COT/SKID* HU16 11 G5
The Crescent *BR/NC/SC* HU15 45 F3
CHULLW HU3 * 35 E4
Cresswell Cl *CHULLN* HU2 36 A1
Creyke Cl *COT/SKID* HU16 11 H4
Creyke La *BR/NC/SC* HU15 45 F3
Crinan Dr *HULLN* HU6 13 F3
Crispin Cl *ANLPK/PPK* HU4 49 G2
Croft Dr *ANL/KKEL* HU10 32 C4
Crofters Dr *COT/SKID* HU16 12 A5
Crofton Av *SINGS* HU8 * 36 C1
Croft Pk *NF/SW* HU14 46 C2
The Croft *BEV* HU17 4 B2
BRAN HU7 14 A3
Croft Vw *ANL/KKEL* HU10 32 C3
BRAN HU7 15 E4
Cromarty Cl *HULLE* HU9 26 A3
Cromer St *SUL/NEW* HU5 23 H4
Crompton Vls *HULLE* HU9 * 37 G1
Cromwell Cl *CHULLW* HU3 35 H1
Cromwell Ct *ANL/KKEL* HU10 33 E2
Cromwell Rd *HEDON* HU12 41 F4
Cropton Rd *SUL/NEW* HU5 22 C4
Crossall Hill La *BR/NC/SC* HU15 45 G3
Crossfield Rd *ANLPK/PPK* HU4 34 B4
HESSLE HU13 49 E1
Crosskill Cl *BEV* HU17 5 F4
Crossland Av *HULLE* HU9 * 37 F1
Cross St *BEV* HU17 4 D5
BRWUH DN19 55 E4
CHULLS HU1 2 B3
Crosswood Cl *BRAN* HU7 9 G3
Crowland Cl *SINGS* HU8 16 C4
Crowle St *HULLE* HU9 37 F2
Crown Ter *BEV* HU17 * 6 D1
Crowther Cl *BEV* HU17 5 F3
Crowther Ct *NF/SW* HU14 * 31 E4
Crowther Wy *NF/SW* HU14 31 E4
Croyland Av *HULLE* HU9 * 37 F1
Crusoe Ct *SUL/NEW* HU5 * 22 C4
Crystal St *CHULLW* HU3 35 G2
Cudworth Gv *SINGS* HU8 24 D5
Cullen Cl *SINGS* HU8 25 E1
Cullingworth Av *HULLN* HU6 13 G4
Cumberland St *CHULLN* HU2 36 C1
Cumberland Vls *SINGS* HU8 * 36 C1
Cumbrian Wy *BRAN* HU7 9 F3
Cundall Cl *HULLE* HU9 25 G5
Curlew Cl *BEV* HU17 4 D2
BRAN HU7 15 F3
Curlew Ct *BTNUH* DN18 52 C4
Curtis Cl *BTNUH* DN18 53 E5
Curzon St *CHULLW* HU3 34 D2
Cuthbert Av *CHULLW* HU3 * 35 F4
Cyprus St *HULLE* HU9 38 B2

D

Dagger La *CHULLS* HU1 2
Dairycoates Av *CHULLW* HU3 35
Dairycoates Rd
ANLPK/PPK HU4 50
Daisyfield Dr *SPR/BIL* HU11 16
Dalby Gv *HULLE* HU9 26
Dale Cl *NF/SW* HU14 31
Dalehouse Dr *ANL/KKEL* HU10 * 33
Dale Rd *BR/NC/SC* HU15 43
NF/SW HU14 31
The Dales *COT/SKID* HU16 10
HULLE HU9 26
Dalesway *ANL/KKEL* HU10 32
Dalkeith Cl *BRAN* HU7 9
Dalsetter Ri *SINGS* HU8 15
Dalton St *SINGS* HU8 24
Dalwood Cl *BRAN* HU7 14
Dam Green La *BR/NC/SC* HU15 44
Dam Rd *BTNUH* DN18 52
Danbury Pk *BRAN* HU7 14
Danby Cl *SINGS* HU8 15
Danepark Rd *HULLN* HU6 12
Danes Dr *HESSLE* HU13 49
Danesway *BEV* HU17 4
Dann Ct *HEDON* HU12 41
Dansom La North *SINGS* HU8 24
Dansom La South *SINGS* HU8 3
Danson Cl *BTNUH* DN18 53
Danthorpe Gv *HULLE* HU9 25
Danube Rd *SUL/NEW* HU5 34
Darnholm Ct *SINGS* HU8 15
Darrell Ct *HEDON* HU12 41
Darrismere Vls *CHULLW* HU3 35
Dart Gv *SINGS* HU8 26
Datchet Garth *ANLPK/PPK* HU4 49
Davenport Av *HESSLE* HU13 48
David's Cl *COT/SKID* HU16 10
Davidstow Cl *BRAN* HU7 14
David Whitfield Cl
CHULLW HU3 34
Daville Cl *SUL/NEW* HU5 21
Davis's Cl *ANL/KKEL* HU10 32
Dawnay Dr *ANL/KKEL* HU10 33
Dawnay Rd *SPR/BIL* HU11 17
Dawson Dr *HULLN* HU6 13
Dayton Rd *SUL/NEW* HU5 22
Deal Cl *SINGS* HU8 15
Deans Dr *SINGS* HU8 25
Dearne Ct *BR/NC/SC* HU15 45
Dearne Gv *SINGS* HU8 25
Deben Gv *SINGS* HU8 16
Deepdale Gv *HULLE* HU9 37
Deerhurst Gv *BRAN* HU7 14
Deer Park Wy *BEV* HU17 6
Dee St *CHULLW* HU3 35
De Grey St *SUL/NEW* HU5 23
De La Pole Av *CHULLW* HU3 34
Delaware Av *CHULLW* HU3 * 34
Delhi St *HULLE* HU9 38
Delius Cl *ANLPK/PPK* HU4 33
The Dell *BEV* HU17 7
Dene Cl *HULLN* HU6 13
Dene Rd *COT/SKID* HU16 11
Dene St *HULLE* HU9 25
Denesway *HESSLE* HU13 48
Denholme Av *HULLN* HU6 13
Denmark Ct *HULLE* HU9 3
Dennett Rd *BEV* HU17 5
Denton St *BEV* HU17 7
Dent Rd *SUL/NEW* HU5 22
Derby St *CHULLW* HU3 35
Derringham Av
ANLPK/PPK HU4 33
Derringham St *CHULLW* HU3 35
Derrymore Rd *ANL/KKEL* HU10 20
Derwent Av *CHULLW* HU3 * 35
NF/SW HU14 46
Derwent Cl *COT/SKID* HU16 12
Derwent Gv *SUL/NEW* HU5 * 23
Derwent St *SINGS* HU8 24
Desmond Av *HULLN* HU6 23
Devon Gv *SUL/NEW* HU5 * 24
Devonport Av *CHULLW* HU3 * 34
Devonshire Vls *CHULLW* HU3 * 35
Devon St *ANLPK/PPK* HU4 50
COT/SKID HU16 12
Dewberry Ct *ANLPK/PPK* HU4 34
Diadem Gv *HULLE* HU9 26
Dibsdane *HULLN* HU6 12
Didscourt *HULLN* HU6 12
Digby Garth *BRAN* HU7 14
Dill Dr *BEV* HU17 7
Dingley Cl *HULLN* HU6 13
Distaff La *HEDON* HU12 40
Ditmas Av *ANLPK/PPK* HU4 33
Division Rd *CHULLW* HU3 35
Dixon Ct *COT/SKID* HU16 21
Dock Office Rw *CHULLS* HU1 2
Dock St *CHULLS* HU1 2
Dodswell Gv *HULLE* HU9 39
Dodthorpe *HULLN* HU6 12
Dog & Duck La *BEV* HU17 4
Dominican Wk *BEV* HU17 7
Doncaster St *CHULLW* HU3 35
Doon Garth *ANLPK/PPK* HU4 49
Dorado Cl *CHULLW* HU3 35
Dorchester Rd *BRAN* HU7 14
Doris V *CHULLW* HU3 * 35
Dorking Cl *SINGS* HU8 26
Dornoch Dr *SINGS* HU8 25
Dorothy Gv *CHULLW* HU3 * 34
Dorset St *ANLPK/PPK* HU4 50
Dorsey Wy *BR/NC/SC* HU15 44
Douglas Rd *SINGS* HU8 16
Dovedale Gv *HULLE* HU9 37
Dover Crs *SUL/NEW* HU5 * 24
Dover St *CHULLW* HU3 35
Dower Ri *NF/SW* HU14 31
Downfield Av *HULLN* HU6 13
Downhill Dr *BRAN* HU7 15
Downing Gv *HULLE* HU9 26
Downs Crs *SUL/NEW* HU5 22
Draper's La *HEDON* HU12 40
Drayton Cl *SINGS* HU8 26
Dressay Gv *SINGS* HU8 15
Driffield Cl *COT/SKID* HU16 11

Guillemot Cl ANLPK/PPK HU4 50 B2
Gullane Dr HULLN HU6 13 F2
Guy Garth HEDON HU12 41 F3
Guy's Crs SINGS HU8 26 A1

H

Hackforth Wk SUL/NEW HU5 22 B2
Hackness Gv SUL/NEW HU5 34 B1
Haddon St CHULLW HU3 34 D5
Hadleigh Cl CHULLN HU2 24 A5
Haggs La ANL/KKEL HU10 21 E3
Hainsworth Pk HULLN HU6 22 C1
Haldane Ct ANLPK/PPK HU4 50 B2
Haldenby Ct NF/SW HU14 * 31 E5
Halecroft Pk BRAN HU7 13 H1
Hales Crs HEDON HU12 40 C4
Hales Entry HULLE HU9 3 J4
Haller St HULLE HU9 37 G1
Hallgarth Wy BEV HU17 7 E1
Hallgate COT/SKID HU16 11 G5
Halliwell Cl HULLE HU9 39 E1
Hall Pk NF/SW HU14 31 G4
Hall Rd HULLN HU6 22 C1
SPR/BIL HU11 19 E1
Hall St CHULLN HU2 35 H2
Hall Wk BR/NC/SC HU15 45 F2
COT/SKID HU16 11 H5
Haltemprice St CHULLW HU3 34 D4
Halyard Cft CHULLS HU1 2 C6
Hambledon Cl BRAN HU7 14 D5
Hambling Dr BEV HU17 4 D2
Hamburg Rd BRAN HU7 24 C1
Hamilton Dr SINGS HU8 15 H5
Hamling Wy ANLPK/PPK HU4 50 B2
Hamlyn Av ANLPK/PPK HU4 34 C2
Hamlyn Dr ANLPK/PPK HU4 34 C3
Hammersmith Rd SINGS HU8 25 H1
Hammond Rd BEV HU17 5 F4
Hampshire St ANLPK/PPK HU4 50 C1
Hampstead Ct CHULLW HU3 23 H5
Hampston Cl HULLN HU6 13 E4
Hamshaw Ct CHULLW HU3 35 G5
Hanley Rd SUL/NEW HU5 22 B3
Hanover Ct BEV HU17 5 F5
CHULLS HU1 2 A4
Hanover Dr BR/NC/SC HU15 * 44 D5
Hanover Sq CHULLS HU1 2 D3
Ha'Penny Bridge Wy
HULLE HU9 3 G5
Harbour Wy HULLE HU9 3 J4
Harcourt Dr HULLE HU9 37 E1
Hardane HULLN HU6 12 C3
Hardington Cl SINGS HU8 16 B4
Hardwick Av SUL/NEW HU5 * 35 F1
Hardwick St SUL/NEW HU5 35 F1
Hardys Rd HEDON HU12 40 C4
Hardy St SUL/NEW HU5 23 G3
Harewood BEV HU17 4 A3
Harewood Av HULLE HU9 26 A3
Harewood Crest
BR/NC/SC HU15 * 45 E5
Hargreave Cl BEV HU17 4 D3
Harland Rd BR/NC/SC HU15 44 D2
Harland Wy COT/SKID HU16 10 D3
Harlech Cl BRAN HU7 9 F4
Harleigh Av BRAN HU7 24 D1
Harlequin Dr BRAN HU7 9 F5
Harleston Cl SINGS HU8 26 B1
Harley St CHULLW HU3 36 A1
Harlow Cl SINGS HU8 16 C5
Harome Gv SUL/NEW HU5 34 A2
Harpham Gv HULLE HU9 26 A5
Harpings Rd SUL/NEW HU5 22 D5
Harrier Rd BTNUH DN18 53 F2
Harrington Ct HEDON HU12 41 F4
Harrison Cl SPR/BIL HU11 19 E1
Harris St CHULLW HU3 34 D4
Harrowdyke BTNUH DN18 52 D4
Harrow St CHULLW HU3 35 F5
Harry's Av SINGS HU8 24 C3
Harthill Dr CHULLW HU3 35 G4
Hartland Cl BRAN HU7 14 B3
Hartley Br HULLE HU9 3 H4
Hartoft Rd SUL/NEW HU5 22 C4
Hartsholme Pk BRAN HU7 14 A1
Harvest Av BTNUH DN18 52 D5
Harvest Ri BRWUH DN19 54 D4
Harwood Dr ANLPK/PPK HU4 33 H3
Haslemere Av SUL/NEW HU5 * 23 H4
Hastings Av SUL/NEW HU5 24 A4
Hastings Gv SUL/NEW HU5 34 C2
Hathersage Rd SINGS HU8 25 E2
Haugh Pk BRAN HU7 13 G1
Hauxwell Gv SINGS HU8 25 H1
Havelock St CHULLW HU3 35 E5
Haven Av BR/NC/SC HU15 44 B4
Haven Basin Rd HEDON HU12 40 D5
Haven Garth BR/NC/SC HU15 44 B4
HEDON HU12 41 F3
Haven Rd BTNUH DN18 52 C3
Havenside HEDON HU12 40 C5
Haven Staithes HEDON HU12 40 D4
The Haven BEV HU17 6 A4
HULLE HU9 3 G4
Haverflats Cl SUL/NEW HU5 22 D5
Hawkesbury St SINGS HU8 25 G3
Hawkshead Gn
ANLPK/PPK HU4 34 A2
Haworth St HULLN HU6 23 G2
Hawthorn Av CHULLW HU3 34 D3
Hawthorn Ct CHULLW HU3 34 D3
Hawthorne Av ANL/KKEL HU10 20 D5
Hawthorne Ct CHULLW HU3 * 34 D3
Hawthorne Garth BEV HU17 5 E3
Hawthorne Ri HESSLE HU13 48 B1
Hawthorn Ga BTNUH DN18 53 F5
Hawthorn Ri BRWUH DN19 54 D4
The Hawthorns SINGS HU8 15 G4
Hayburn Av SUL/NEW HU5 22 C4
Haydock Garth BRAN HU7 14 C1
Haydon Cl ANL/KKEL HU10 32 D1
Hayes Av SUL/NEW HU5 * 23 F4
Haymarket Cl SINGS HU8 25 H2
Haymer Dr HEDON HU12 41 F4
Hayton Gv ANLPK/PPK HU4 34 C5
Hayward Cl BEV HU17 6 A4
Hazelbarrow Dr
ANL/KKEL HU10 33 F2
Hazel Ct BR/NC/SC HU15 * 44 D4
Hazel Gv CHULLW HU3 35 H4
Headlands Dr HESSLE HU13 48 C2
Heads La HESSLE HU13 48 C2
Heathcote St HULLN HU6 23 H2
Heather Cl SUL/NEW HU5 34 B1
Heatherwood Ct BRAN HU7 15 E2
Hebden Av SINGS HU8 26 B1
Hebrides Cl HULLE HU9 26 A3
Hedgerow Cl BRWUH DN19 54 D4
Hedgerow Ct HULLN HU6 13 F3
Hedley Cl BR/NC/SC HU15 42 B3
Hedon Rd HULLE HU9 3 H3
HULLE HU9 37 H2
Hellyers Ct ANLPK/PPK HU4 50 B2
Helm Dr HULLE HU9 3 K3
Helms Av HEDON HU12 28 D5
Helmsdale HULLE HU9 * 25 F5
Helmsley Gv SUL/NEW HU5 34 A2
Helsinki Rd BRAN HU7 24 B1
Helvellyn Cl BRAN HU7 9 G5
Hemble Wy BRAN HU7 14 A1
Hemmingway Wk
HESSLE HU13 48 D1
Hemswell Av HULLE HU9 38 D1
Hengate BEV HU17 4 D5
Henley Av HULLE HU9 * 37 E1
Henley Dr HULLE HU9 25 G5
Henley Vls SUL/NEW HU5 * 23 H4
Henry Boot Wy
ANLPK/PPK HU4 49 H3
Henson Vls SUL/NEW HU5 * 23 H5
Hepworth Ar CHULLS HU1 * 2 E4
Hereford Cl BEV HU17 6 D3
Hereford St ANLPK/PPK HU4 50 C1
Hermes Cl HULLE HU9 26 C2
Heron Cl HEDON HU12 40 C4
Heron St CHULLW HU3 35 F4
Heron Wy BTNUH DN18 52 C4
Hertfordshire Cl SUL/NEW HU5 22 B5
Heslerton Av COT/SKID HU16 21 G2
Hessle Rd ANLPK/PPK HU4 49 H2
CHULLW HU3 35 E5
HESSLE HU13 49 G2
Hessle Vw BTNUH DN18 52 C4
Hewson's La BTNUH DN18 52 D2
Hickling Cl ANL/KKEL HU10 33 G3
Higham Cl SINGS HU8 15 G4
Higham Wy BR/NC/SC HU15 45 E4
Highcourt HULLN HU6 12 C4
Highdales ANL/KKEL HU10 32 C1
High Farm Ct SPR/BIL HU11 17 F4
Highfield BRAN HU7 15 F5
Highfield Cl BRAN HU7 15 F5
Highfield Crs BTNUH DN18 53 F4
SPR/BIL HU11 17 F4
Highfield Ri HEDON HU12 29 E4
Highfield Rd BEV HU17 5 E3
Highfields BR/NC/SC HU15 43 E2
BRWUH DN19 54 D4
Highfield Wy NF/SW HU14 46 C4
Highgate BEV HU17 7 E1
Highgate Cl SINGS HU8 26 A1
Highgate Ct BEV HU17 * 7 E1
Highgrove Wy BRAN HU7 9 E5
High Hunsley Circuit
COT/SKID HU16 10 A2
High Hunsley Circuit &
Beverley 20 COT/SKID HU16 10 A4
High Mdw ANL/KKEL HU10 32 C1
High Rd BR/NC/SC HU15 42 A1
BR/NC/SC HU15 45 E1
High St BRWUH DN19 55 E4
BTNUH DN18 52 D3
CHULLS HU1 2 E5
NF/SW HU14 46 C3
High Trees Mt BRAN HU7 15 G5
Hilary Gv ANLPK/PPK HU4 49 H2
Hildyard Cl ANL/KKEL HU10 33 F3
HEDON HU12 41 E4
Hill Brow ANL/KKEL HU10 32 B3
Hillcrest BEV HU17 4 B3
Hillcrest Av HESSLE HU13 48 C2
Hillcrest Dr BEV HU17 4 C2
Hillman Rd HESSLE HU13 49 F1
Hill Ri BR/NC/SC HU15 44 C2
Hillside Dr BTNUH DN18 52 C4
Hill St SINGS HU8 24 C4
Hillsway Cl SINGS HU8 25 F2
Hilston Gv HULLE HU9 26 B5
Hinderwell St SUL/NEW HU5 23 G5
Hirncroft Cl SINGS HU8 15 G4
Hobart St CHULLW HU3 2 A5
Hobson Rd BR/NC/SC HU15 44 D2
Hodder Gv SINGS HU8 16 C5
Hodge Ct HULLE HU9 3 K1
Hodgson Av BEV HU17 5 E4
Hodgson St SINGS HU8 2 E1
Hogg La ANL/KKEL HU10 32 B1
Holborn St HULLE HU9 3 G1
Holbrook Cl BRAN HU7 24 D2
Holcombe Cl SINGS HU8 16 B4
Holcroft Garth HEDON HU12 41 E3
Holderness Ar HULLE HU9 * 3 F1
Holderness Crs BEV HU17 5 E5
Holderness Rd HULLE HU9 3 H1
Holderness Vls CHULLW HU3 * 35 E4
HULLE HU9 * 38 C2
Holgate Cl BEV HU17 5 G5
Holgate Pl NF/SW HU14 31 F4
Holland St HULLE HU9 25 E5
Holland Wy HULLE HU9 3 J2
The Hollies ANL/KKEL HU10 21 E4
BEV HU17 5 F2
SUL/NEW HU5 * 23 G3
Holly Bush Wy BEV HU17 4 C5
Holly Dr COT/SKID HU16 21 E1
Holly Gv SINGS HU8 25 E4
Holly Hl BR/NC/SC HU15 45 G3
Hollytree Av SUL/NEW HU5 33 H2
Holme Church La BEV HU17 7 F1
Holme Crs COT/SKID HU16 11 E5
Holmes La SPR/BIL HU11 17 G4
Holm Garth Dr SINGS HU8 26 B1
Holwell Rd BRAN HU7 24 C1
Holwick Ms SUL/NEW HU5 22 B2
Holydyke BTNUH DN18 52 D4
Holyrood Av CHULLW HU3 * 34 D2
HULLE HU9 * 37 E1
Holyrood Vls HULLE HU9 * 25 F5
Home Cl ANLPK/PPK HU4 34 A4
Home Gn COT/SKID HU16 21 G1
Homethorpe HULLN HU6 13 E3
Honeysuckle Pl
BR/NC/SC HU15 44 D4
Honiton Rd BRAN HU7 14 C3
Honley Wood Cl BRAN HU7 15 F2
Hood St SINGS HU8 36 C1
Hopewell Rd HULLE HU9 26 B3
Hop Gv SUL/NEW HU5 * 23 G4
Hopkins St HULLE HU9 26 A3
Hopwood Cl CHULLW HU3 35 H1
Hornbeam Dr COT/SKID HU16 22 A1
Hornbeams Ct BRAN HU7 15 F5
Hornbeam Wk COT/SKID HU16 21 H1
Hornby Gv HULLE HU9 26 C3
Hornscroft Pk BRAN HU7 13 G1
Hornsea Rail Trail
& Trans Pennine Trail
BRAN HU7 15 H2
HULLE HU9 * 3 F1
Hornsea Vls SUL/NEW HU5 * 24 A4
Hotham Dr SUL/NEW HU5 33 H1
Hotham Rd North
SUL/NEW HU5 22 C3
Hotham Rd South
SUL/NEW HU5 33 H1
Hotham Sq BEV HU17 5 G5
Hotham St HULLE HU9 37 F2
Hotton Cl HULLE HU9 26 C5
The Hourne HESSLE HU13 49 E2
Housemartin Dr SINGS HU8 15 G3
Houston Dr SUL/NEW HU5 23 H3
Hove Rd SUL/NEW HU5 22 B5
Hovingham Cl SINGS HU8 15 G4
Howdale Rd SINGS HU8 15 G5
Howsham Cl HULLE HU9 26 D1
Hoylake Cl COT/SKID HU16 22 C1
Hucknall Garth BRAN HU7 14 D2
Hudson Gdns SUL/NEW HU5 23 H5
Hudson St CHULLW HU3 35 H1
Hudson Wy BEV HU17 4 B1
Hull Bridge Rd BEV HU17 5 E3
Hull Rd ANL/KKEL HU10 33 E3
BEV HU17 7 G1
COT/SKID HU16 22 B1
HEDON HU12 40 A3
HESSLE HU13 49 F3
HULLE HU9 39 F2
SPR/BIL HU11 17 E1
Humber Br HESSLE HU13 48 C5
Humber Crs BR/NC/SC HU15 44 D4
Humberdale Cl NF/SW HU14 31 F5
Humberdale Dr NF/SW HU14 47 G4
Humber Dock St CHULLS HU1 2 C5
Humber Pl CHULLS HU1 2 D6
Humber Rd BTNUH DN18 52 D2
NF/SW HU14 46 D5
Humber St CHULLS HU1 2 D6
Humber Vw BTNUH DN18 52 C4
HESSLE HU13 48 C2
NF/SW HU14 31 F5
Humbleton Rd HEDON HU12 19 H5
Hungate BTNUH DN18 52 D3
Hungerhills Dr SPR/BIL HU11 17 G4
Hunsley Av SUL/NEW HU5 21 H5
Hunter Cl HEDON HU12 29 E5
Hunter Gv CHULLW HU3 35 E5
Hunter Rd BR/NC/SC HU15 44 C3
Huntingdon St ANLPK/PPK HU4 50 C1
Huntley Dr SUL/NEW HU5 23 E5
Hurley Cl SINGS HU8 25 H3
Hurn Cl SINGS HU8 15 G5
Hurn Vw BEV HU17 4 C4
Husthwaite Rd BR/NC/SC HU15 45 E5
Hutton Cl SUL/NEW HU5 22 C4
Hutt St CHULLW HU3 35 H2
Huzzard Cl BEV HU17 6 A4
Hykeham Cl BRAN HU7 9 F5
Hymers Av CHULLW HU3 35 F2
Hyperion St HULLE HU9 3 F2
Hytec Wy BR/NC/SC HU15 44 B4

I

Icehouse Rd CHULLW HU3 35 H3
Idas Cl HULLE HU9 3 F5
Ilchester Cl BRAN HU7 14 D5
Ilford Rd SUL/NEW HU5 22 A5
Ilkley Vls HULLE HU9 * 37 F1
Ilthorpe HULLN HU6 13 E3
Impala Wy ANLPK/PPK HU4 50 B1
Imperial Ct HULLE HU9 26 A3
Ingland Ct HULLE HU9 26 B5
Ingleby Cl SINGS HU8 15 H4
Inglefield Cl BEV HU17 6 B5
Inglemire Av HULLN HU6 23 G2
Inglemire La COT/SKID HU16 22 B1
Ingleton BR/NC/SC HU15 44 D3
Ingleton Av ANLPK/PPK HU4 34 A3
Inglewood Dr ANLPK/PPK HU4 33 H3
Ingmires BR/NC/SC HU15 * 45 F3
Ingram Av SPR/BIL HU11 17 F5
Ings La BR/NC/SC HU15 44 C5
HULLN HU6 8 A5
NF/SW HU14 46 D5
Ings Rd BEV HU17 4 C1
BRAN HU7 25 F1
SINGS HU8 25 H2
Inmans Rd HEDON HU12 41 E3
Innescourt HULLN HU6 12 C4
Innsworth Garth BRAN HU7 14 D2
Inverewe Wy COT/SKID HU16 21 F1
Iona Cl SINGS HU8 15 G4
Irene Av SINGS HU8 * 25 E5
SUL/NEW HU5 * 35 E1
Irene Gv CHULLW HU3 * 35 F4
Irenes Av SINGS HU8 * 24 D3
Isis Ct HULLE HU9 3 G5
Isledane HULLN HU6 12 C3
Itlings La HESSLE HU13 49 F3
Ivanhoe Vls HULLE HU9 * 37 G1
Iveson Cl HEDON HU12 40 D3
Ivydene Vls HULLE HU9 * 37 F1
Ivy Gv SUL/NEW HU5 * 35 E1
Ivy La HEDON HU12 40 D3
Ivyleigh Av CHULLW HU3 * 34 D3
Ivy Ter SINGS HU8 * 24 D5
Ivy Vls HULLE HU9 * 37 F1

J

Jackson St CHULLW HU3 35 H5
Jack Taylor La BEV HU17 7 G1
Jade Gv CHULLW HU3 35 E5
Jalland St SINGS HU8 25 E5
James Niven Ct HULLE HU9 25 F5
Jameson St CHULLS HU1 2 C3
Jameson Vls SUL/NEW HU5 * 23 H3
James Reckitt Av SINGS HU8 24 D5
Jarratt St CHULLS HU1 2 C2
Jasmine Gv BRAN HU7 14 B1
Jason Garth BRAN HU7 15 E2
Jefferson Cl BEV HU17 4 D3
Jefferson Ct HULLE HU9 * 37 E1
Jefferson Dr BR/NC/SC HU15 44 B3
Jendale BRAN HU7 14 B3
Jenning St SINGS HU8 36 C1
Jenny Brough La HESSLE HU13 48 C1
Jenny Brough Mdw
HESSLE HU13 48 B1
Jenthorpe HULLN HU6 13 E3
Jervis Rd HULLE HU9 26 D1
Jesmond Dene HULLE HU9 * 25 F5
Jesmond Gdns HULLE HU9 25 F5
Jesmond Rd COT/SKID HU16 12 A5
Jetcourt HULLN HU6 12 C4
Jill Gv HESSLE HU13 49 F3
Jipdane HULLN HU6 12 D3
Jobsons Cl BR/NC/SC HU15 42 B3
John Gray Ct ANL/KKEL HU10 20 D5
John Harrison's Cl
BRWUH DN19 55 E3
John Newton Wy BRAN HU7 13 H2
Johnston Ct BEV HU17 4 C2
John St CHULLN HU2 2 C2
Joscelyn Av BRAN HU7 24 D1
Jubilee Sq CHULLN HU2 2 D1
Julian Cl SUL/NEW HU5 33 G2
Julians Wk ANL/KKEL HU10 33 F3
Juliet Reckitt Hvn SINGS HU8 * 25 E3
Junella Cl CHULLW HU3 35 E5
Juniper Cha BEV HU17 4 C5

K

Kathleen Rd SINGS HU8 24 D4
Katrine Cl BRAN HU7 25 F1
Keble Gv HULLE HU9 26 A5
Kedrum Rd HULLE HU9 25 H5
Keel Ct BEV HU17 7 G1
Keel Rd HULLN HU6 13 G3
Kelberdale Cl BRAN HU7 9 E5
Keld Cl HEDON HU12 41 F4
Keldgate BEV HU17 6 D1
Keldgate Bar BEV HU17 6 D2
Keldgate Cl BEV HU17 6 D1
Keldgate Rd BEV HU17 6 B2
COT/SKID HU16 10 D4
Kelgate Cl SINGS HU8 15 G4
Kelston Dr HESSLE HU13 49 F1
Kelvin St HULLE HU9 25 G4
Kemp Rd NF/SW HU14 47 E1
Kempton Cl BEV HU17 4 D3
Kempton Rd CHULLW HU3 34 C3
Kendal Wy ANLPK/PPK HU4 34 A2
Kenilworth Av SUL/NEW HU5 22 D3
Kenmore Dr HULLN HU6 13 E2
Kennet Rd SINGS HU8 16 C5
Kennington Wk
COT/SKID HU16 12 B5
Kensington Gv CHULLW HU3 * 35 E3
Kent Cl HULLE HU9 3 K1
Kentmere Cl BRAN HU7 9 G3
Kent Rd COT/SKID HU16 21 G1
Kenwardly Rd ANL/KKEL HU10 33 E1
Kerdane HULLN HU6 12 D3
Kerry Dr ANL/KKEL HU10 32 B3
Kerry Pit Wy ANL/KKEL HU10 32 C3
Kesteven Wy BRAN HU7 14 A1
Kestrel Av BRAN HU7 15 F3
Keswick Gdns HULLN HU6 12 C5
Kettlethorpe Dr
BR/NC/SC HU15 45 F5
Kettlewell Cl BRAN HU7 9 F4
Ketwell La HEDON HU12 40 D3
Kidd La BR/NC/SC HU15 45 F2
Kilburn Av CHULLN HU2 36 A1
Kildale Cl SINGS HU8 15 G5
Kilkoy Dr BRAN HU7 9 E5
Kilnsea Gv HULLE HU9 25 H4
Kilnwick Av SUL/NEW HU5 22 A4
Kilton Ct SINGS HU8 15 G4
Kilvin Dr BEV HU17 5 F3
Kimberley Av CHULLW HU3 * 34 D4
Kimberley St CHULLW HU3 35 G2
Kimmeridge Cl BRAN HU7 14 D5
Kinderscout Cl BRAN HU7 9 F5
King Charles Cl ANL/KKEL HU10 33 E2
King Edwards Ter
BR/NC/SC HU15 44 B4
King Edward St CHULLS HU1 2 B2
Kingfisher Cl BRAN HU7 15 F3
Kingfisher Ri BRAN HU7 15 G5
King's Bench St CHULLW HU3 35 F4
Kingsbury Wy BRAN HU7 9 E5
Kingscott Cl BRAN HU7 14 B2
King's Cross Cl CHULLW HU3 35 G3
Kings Gdns SUL/NEW HU5 * 23 F4
Kings Leigh CHULLW HU3 35 G3
Kingsley Av HULLE HU9 25 G3
Kingsley Cl BR/NC/SC HU15 44 C5
Kingsley Dr ANL/KKEL HU10 20 D5
King's Pl HEDON HU12 41 E3
Kingsport Cl CHULLW HU3 35 E2
King's Sq BEV HU17 5 E4
Kingston Av HESSLE HU13 49 F3
Kingston Pk CHULLS HU1 * 2 A6
Kingston Ri ANL/KKEL HU10 20 C5
Kingston Rd ANL/KKEL HU10 32
Kingston Sq CHULLS HU1 2
Kingston St CHULLS HU1 2
Kingston Vw BTNUH DN18 53
Kingston Vls HULLE HU9 * 37
Kingston Wy BRAN HU7 24
Kingston Whf CHULLS HU1 2
King St BTNUH DN18 53
COT/SKID HU16 11
Kingsway COT/SKID HU16 21
Kingtree Av COT/SKID HU16 11
Kinloss Garth BRAN HU7 15
Kinthorpe HULLN HU6 13
Kiplington Cl CHULLW HU3 35
Kipling Wk ANLPK/PPK HU4 50
Kirby Dr COT/SKID HU16 11
Kirkby St CHULLN HU2 36
Kirk Cl BRAN HU7 15
Kirk Cft COT/SKID HU16 11
Kirkdale Gdns SUL/NEW HU5 * 23
Kirkebie Dr HEDON HU12 41
Kirkham Cl HESSLE HU13 49
Kirkham Dr SUL/NEW HU5 23
Kirkholme Wy BEV HU17 5
Kirklands Rd SUL/NEW HU5 34
Kirk Ri ANL/KKEL HU10 32
Kirk Rd HEDON HU12 28
Kirkstead Av SINGS HU8 * 24
Kirkstead St SINGS HU8 24
Kirkstone Rd SUL/NEW HU5 22
Kirkway ANL/KKEL HU10 32
Kitchen La BEV HU17 6
Knapton Av SUL/NEW HU5 22
Knightly Wy BRAN HU7 13
Knightsbridge Ct CHULLW HU3 23
Knightscourt HULLN HU6 12
Knights Wy BEV HU17 5
Knole Pk BRAN HU7 14
Knowles Av HULLN HU6 13
Knowsley Av COT/SKID HU16 11
Kottingham Av SUL/NEW HU5 23
Kyffin Av HULLE HU9 26
Kyle Cl SINGS HU8 16

L

Laburnum Av SINGS HU8 25
SUL/NEW HU5 * 23
Laburnum Dr BEV HU17 5
SUL/NEW HU5 33
Laburnum Gv SINGS HU8 * 24
Ladybower Cl SINGS HU8 15
Ladygate BEV HU17 4
Ladyside Cl BRAN HU7 9
Ladysmith Rd ANL/KKEL HU10 21
Ladywell Ga BR/NC/SC HU15 45
Lagoon Dr BRAN HU7 15
Lairgate BEV HU17 4
Lake Dr SINGS HU8 25
Lakeside Gv ANLPK/PPK HU4 34
Lake Vw SINGS HU8 25
Lambert Av BR/NC/SC HU15 44
Lambert Park Rd HEDON HU12 40
Lambert St SUL/NEW HU5 23
Lambton St SUL/NEW HU5 23
Lambwath Hall Ct BRAN HU7 15
Lambwath Rd SINGS HU8 25
Lamorna Av SINGS HU8 24
Lanark St SUL/NEW HU5 35
Lancaster Dr SINGS HU8 25
Lancaster Wy BR/NC/SC HU15 44
Lancelot Ct HULLE HU9 3
Land of Green Ginger
CHULLS HU1 2
Landress La BEV HU17 6
Langdale Av BEV HU17 5
SUL/NEW HU5 22
Langdale Crs COT/SKID HU16 21
Langford Wk ANLPK/PPK HU4 33
Langholm Cl BEV HU17 4
Langley Pk BRAN HU7 9
Langsett Rd SINGS HU8 15
Langthwaite Cl
BR/NC/SC HU15 45
Langtoft Gv HULLN HU6 12
Langtree Cl BRAN HU7 14
Lansdowne St CHULLW HU3 35
Lanyon Cl BRAN HU7 15
Lapwing Cl BRAN HU7 15
Lapwing Wy BTNUH DN18 52
Larard Av HULLN HU6 13
Larch Cl SUL/NEW HU5 23
Larchmont Cl BR/NC/SC HU15 44
Larne Rd HULLE HU9 26
Lashbrook Garth
ANLPK/PPK HU4 33
Lastingham BR/NC/SC HU15 44
Lastingham Cl HULLN HU6 12
Laughton Rd BEV HU17 5
Laurel Av SUL/NEW HU5 * 35
Laurel Cl SUL/NEW HU5 33
Laurel Ct BEV HU17 4
Laurel Gv CHULLW HU3 * 35
The Laurels SUL/NEW HU5 * 23
Laurel Vls HULLE HU9 * 37
Lavender Cl BRAN HU7 14
Lavender Wk BEV HU17 6
SUL/NEW HU5 34
Lawnsgarth COT/SKID HU16 11
The Lawns ANL/KKEL HU10 32
BEV HU17 4
BRAN HU7 15
Lawnswood HESSLE HU13 48
Lawnswood Cl BRAN HU7 25
Lawrence Av SINGS HU8 25
Lawson Av COT/SKID HU16 11
Lawson Cl HULLN HU6 23
Laxthorpe HULLN HU6 13
Laxton Garth ANL/KKEL HU10 20
L B Av CHULLW HU3 * 35
Lea Crs COT/SKID HU16 21
Leadhills Wy BRAN HU7 15
Leads Rd BRAN HU7 24
Lealholm Ct SINGS HU8 15
Lealholme Ct SINGS HU8 * 15
Leame Cl CHULLW HU3 35
Leander Rd HULLE HU9 26

Novello Garth ANLPK/PPK HU4 33 H5
Nunburnholme Av NF/SW HU14 46 C4
Nunburnholme Pk SUL/NEW HU5 33 H2
Nunnery Wk BR/NC/SC HU15 42 B3
Nunnington Cl SUL/NEW HU5 23 F4
The Nurseries BEV HU17 4 C3
Nursery Cl ANLPK/PPK HU4 33 H4
BTNUH DN18 53 F3
Nursery Ct BR/NC/SC HU15 44 D4
Nursery Gdns BEV HU17 6 D2
Nursery Gv HULLE HU9 26 B4
Nursery La HULLN HU6 22 C2
Nursery Vw COT/SKID HU16 12 A4
Nursery Wk COT/SKID HU16 12 B5
Nuttles La HEDON HU12 29 G2

O

Oak Av ANL/KKEL HU10 20 D5
BR/NC/SC HU15 44 D3
CHULLW HU3 * 34 D2
Oak Cl BEV HU17 5 F3
SPR/BIL HU11 19 E1
Oakdale Av ANL/KKEL HU10 33 E1
Oakdene COT/SKID HU16 21 H1
Oak Dr ANLPK/PPK HU4 33 H2
Oakfield Ct HULLN HU6 22 D2
Oak Gv BRWUH DN19 54 D5
HEDON HU12 40 C3
Oak Hl ANL/KKEL HU10 20 C4
Oakington Garth BRAN HU7 15 E3
Oaklands Dr ANL/KKEL HU10 20 C5
HESSLE HU13 48 D1
Oakland Vls SUL/NEW HU5 * 23 G4
Oak Rd HULLN HU6 23 H1
Oaksley Carr BEV HU17 7 H3
Oak Sq BRAN HU7 8 D2
Oak Tree Cl BEV HU17 4 C3
Oak Tree Dr BEV HU17 4 C3
Oaktree Dr SINGS HU8 15 F4
Oak Tree Est HEDON HU12 28 D5
Oakwell Gv SINGS HU8 24 D5
Oakwood Cl SUL/NEW HU5 33 G2
Oban Av CHULLW HU3 * 34 D2
HULLE HU9 26 A4
Occupation La NF/SW HU14 31 F1
Ocean Bvd HULLE HU9 3 G4
The Octagon ANL/KKEL HU10 32 D1
Old Annandale Rd ANL/KKEL HU10 32 C1
Oldbeck Rd BEV HU17 5 H5
Old Dairy BRWUH DN19 55 F4
Oldfield Av HULLN HU6 13 G5
Old Manor Lawns BEV HU17 7 E1
Old Pond Pl NF/SW HU14 46 D5
The Old Stables BEV HU17 * 4 C5
Oldstead Av HULLN HU6 22 D1
Old Waste BEV HU17 * 4 D5
Olivier Ct ANLPK/PPK HU4 50 C1
On Hl NF/SW HU14 31 F4
Onyx Gv CHULLW HU3 35 E5
Orchard Cl ANL/KKEL HU10 33 F2
BEV HU17 4 C4
BRWUH DN19 54 D5
BTNUH DN18 53 F5
Orchard Cft COT/SKID HU16 11 H3
Orchard Dr HESSLE HU13 49 E3
Orchard Garth BEV HU17 4 C3
Orchard Park Rd COT/SKID HU16 12 B3
Orchard Rd COT/SKID HU16 10 A3
The Orchard HULLE HU9 26 B2
Oribi Cl ANLPK/PPK HU4 50 A2
Oriel Cl BEV HU17 6 A4
Oriel Gv HULLE HU9 26 A5
Orion Cl CHULLW HU3 35 F4
Orkney Cl SINGS HU8 15 G5
Ormerod Crs SUL/NEW HU5 22 B4
Ormerod Rd SUL/NEW HU5 22 B4
Ormington Vls HULLE HU9 * 3 J1
Ormonde Av HULLN HU6 23 H2
Orniscourt HULLN HU6 12 D4
Orpington Vls HULLE HU9 * 25 F5
Osborne St CHULLS HU1 2 A4
Oslo Rd BRAN HU7 14 B5
Osprey Cl HULLN HU6 13 F3
Otley Cl HULLE HU9 26 C4
Ottawa Cl COT/SKID HU16 21 F1
Otterburn St CHULLW HU3 35 E4
Outer Trinities BEV HU17 7 E1
Outlands Rd COT/SKID HU16 22 B1
Outram Cl CHULLN HU2 36 A1
Oval Rd ANLPK/PPK HU4 33 H4
The Oval ANL/KKEL HU10 33 E1
BR/NC/SC HU15 44 D3
SINGS HU8 25 E4
Overland Rd COT/SKID HU16 22 A1
Overstrand Dr BRAN HU7 15 F5
Overton Av ANL/KKEL HU10 21 E5
Overton Ct BTNUH DN18 52 D3
Owbridge Ct CHULLS HU1 * 2 A4
Owen Av HESSLE HU13 49 G3
Owston Pk HULLN HU6 22 C1
Owthorne Vls HULLE HU9 * 37 F1
Oxenhope Rd HULLN HU6 13 H4
Oxford Cl BEV HU17 6 D3
Oxford St CHULLN HU2 36 C1
Oxford Violet BRAN HU7 14 A4

P

Packman La ANL/KKEL HU10 32 B1
Paddock Ri BRWUH DN19 54 D4
The Paddocks ANL/KKEL HU10 32 B2
The Paddock ANLPK/PPK HU4 33 H4
BEV HU17 4 C3
COT/SKID HU16 12 A5
NF/SW HU14 31 G4
NF/SW HU14 46 C2
Paddock Vw SPR/BIL HU11 18 A5
Padstow Cl BRAN HU7 14 B2
Paisley St CHULLW HU3 35 E3
Palmcourt HULLN HU6 12 D4
Palmer Av ANL/KKEL HU10 32 D1
Palmer La BRWUH DN19 55 E4
The Parade SUL/NEW HU5 23 H5
Paradise Sq BEV HU17 * 7 E1
Paragon Ar CHULLS HU1 * 2 B3
Paragon Sq CHULLS HU1 2 B3
Paragon St CHULLS HU1 2 B3
Parcevall Dr BRAN HU7 14 A2
Park Av BEV HU17 4 D4
BTNUH DN18 52 D4
CHULLW HU3 * 35 E3
COT/SKID HU16 11 G4
HESSLE HU13 49 E1
SUL/NEW HU5 23 F5
Park Av West SUL/NEW HU5 23 E5
Parkdale BTNUH DN18 52 D5
Parkfield Av NF/SW HU14 46 C4
Parkfield Cots BEV HU17 * 4 C5
Parkfield Dr CHULLW HU3 34 D2
Park Gv HULLE HU9 * 25 F5
SUL/NEW HU5 23 G5
Parkhurst Cl SINGS HU8 26 C1
Parklands Crs NF/SW HU14 46 C3
Parklands Dr NF/SW HU14 46 C3
The Parklands BR/NC/SC HU15 42 D2
Park La COT/SKID HU16 11 F3
SUL/NEW HU5 23 H5
Park La East ANLPK/PPK HU4 34 A3
Park La West ANLPK/PPK HU4 34 A3
Park Rd BR/NC/SC HU15 45 G3
CHULLW HU3 23 H5
SPR/BIL HU11 18 D1
SUL/NEW HU5 23 H5
Park Rw CHULLN HU2 35 H2
SPR/BIL HU11 18 D1
Parkside Cl COT/SKID HU16 11 F5
SUL/NEW HU5 23 F5
Parkstone Rd HULLN HU6 13 G4
Park St CHULLW HU3 35 H3
The Park NF/SW HU14 31 E5
Park Vw ANLPK/PPK HU4 34 C5
BTNUH DN18 53 E5
Park View Cl BRWUH DN19 54 D5
Park Wk ANLPK/PPK HU4 33 H4
BRAN HU7 * 15 F4
The Parkway ANL/KKEL HU10 33 E1
COT/SKID HU16 21 G1
Parliament St BR/NC/SC HU15 45 F3
CHULLS HU1 2 D4
Parnham Dr BRAN HU7 9 E5
Parthian Rd HULLE HU9 26 C3
Pasture La BEV HU17 4 C5
Pasture Rd BTNUH DN18 53 F3
Pasture Rd North BTNUH DN18 53 F3
Pasture Rd South BTNUH DN18 53 G3
Pasture Ter BEV HU17 4 C5
The Pathway CHULLS HU1 * 2 D4
Patrington Garth BRAN HU7 15 E3
Patterdale Rd SUL/NEW HU5 34 C1
Paull Rd HEDON HU12 39 H3
Pavilion Cl SINGS HU8 24 D3
Pavilion Crs SUL/NEW HU5 * 23 H3
Paxdale BRAN HU7 14 A3
Peacehaven Cl BRAN HU7 14 D4
Peace Wk HEDON HU12 28 D5
Peach Tree Ct CHULLW HU3 35 H4
Pearson Av SUL/NEW HU5 23 H4
Pearson St CHULLN HU2 2 A2
Pearson Wy HULLN HU6 24 B3
Pear Tree Cl SINGS HU8 25 E2
Pearts Arch HESSLE HU13 * 49 G2
Peaseholme HESSLE HU13 48 C2
Pease St CHULLW HU3 2 A4
Peckham Cl SINGS HU8 25 G1
Peel Pl BEV HU17 4 C5
CHULLW HU3 35 H1
Peel St CHULLW HU3 35 H1
Pelham Cl BEV HU17 6 D4
BTNUH DN18 52 C5
Pelham Dr HULLE HU9 3 K1
Pemberton Gdns SUL/NEW HU5 * 24 A4
Pemberton St SINGS HU8 3 G1
Pembroke Gv HULLE HU9 25 H5
Pembroke Vls HULLE HU9 * 37 F1
Pendeen Gv SINGS HU8 24 D3
Pendle Cl BRAN HU7 9 G5
Pendrill St CHULLW HU3 23 H5
Penistone Cl HULLE HU9 * 37 F2
Penistone Ct HULLE HU9 37 F2
Pennine Wy BRAN HU7 9 F4
Pennington St SINGS HU8 3 G1
Pennyholme Cl BRAN HU7 9 E5
Pennyman Rd BEV HU17 5 F4
Penrose Cl BRAN HU7 14 B2
Penshurst Av HESSLE HU13 49 F1
Pentland Cl SINGS HU8 15 H4
Penwith Dr ANL/KKEL HU10 33 E2
Peppleton Cl BRAN HU7 25 E2
Percy Cots CHULLW HU3 * 35 G1
Percy St CHULLN HU2 2 B2
Peregrine Cl ANLPK/PPK HU4 50 B2
Perivale Cl SINGS HU8 26 A1
Perran Cl BRAN HU7 14 D4
Perry St CHULLW HU3 35 E3
Perth St SUL/NEW HU5 34 D1
Perth St West SUL/NEW HU5 35 E1
Perth Vls SUL/NEW HU5 * 35 E1
Petersfield Cl BRAN HU7 14 D5
Petersham Cl SINGS HU8 26 A1
Petuaria Cl BR/NC/SC HU15 44 B3
Petula Ct SINGS HU8 15 G4
Pevensey Cl BRAN HU7 14 D4
Philip Larkin Cl HULLN HU6 23 G2
Phoenix Cl SINGS HU8 25 H2
Pickering Crs ANLPK/PPK HU4 * 50 B1
Pickering Rd ANLPK/PPK HU4 50 A1
The Pickerings NF/SW HU14 46 D5
Pickering Vw ANLPK/PPK HU4 50 B1
Pier St CHULLS HU1 2 D6
Pighill La BEV HU17 4 C2
Pilot's Vw BTNUH DN18 52 D1
Pilots Wy HULLE HU9 3 G5
Pinderfield Cl SINGS HU8 16 A5
Pine Mdw ANL/KKEL HU10 32 B1
Pine Wk BR/NC/SC HU15 44 D2
Pinewood Gv SUL/NEW HU5 34 A2
Pinfold BR/NC/SC HU15 42 B3
Pinfold Ct HEDON HU12 28 D5
Pinfold Ms BEV HU17 5 E5
Pioneer Pk HULLN HU6 * 24 C3
Pitman Av BTNUH DN18 52 C5
Pitsford Cl BRAN HU7 14 C2
Pitt St CHULLW HU3 34 D2
Plane St CHULLW HU3 35 E3
Plantation Cl BEV HU17 5 G5
Plantation Dr BR/NC/SC HU15 42 B3
NF/SW HU14 46 B3
Plantation Dr West ANLPK/PPK HU4 34 A3
Plimsoll Wy HULLE HU9 3 H4
Plover Ct BTNUH DN18 52 C3
Plover Dr BR/NC/SC HU15 44 D3
Plowden Rd CHULLW HU3 34 C4
Plum Tree Rd SPR/BIL HU11 19 E1
Plum Tree Wk BR/NC/SC HU15 43 E2
Plym Gv SINGS HU8 16 C5
Polo Vls SUL/NEW HU5 * 35 E1
Ponds Wy BTNUH DN18 52 C3
Poolbank La BR/NC/SC HU15 45 G4
Pools Brook Pk BRAN HU7 13 G1
Poorhouse La HULLE HU9 38 C1
Poplar Av SUL/NEW HU5 * 23 F4
Poplar Cl ANLPK/PPK HU4 33 G4
Poplar Ct BRAN HU7 25 E1
Poplar Dr BEV HU17 5 E3
Poplar Gv HEDON HU12 40 C3
SINGS HU8 * 24 C3
The Poplars SINGS HU8 * 25 E4
SUL/NEW HU5 * 23 F4
Poplars Wy BEV HU17 6 C3
Popple St HULLE HU9 3 G3
Porlock Dr BRAN HU7 14 C2
Port Av HULLN HU6 13 G3
Porter St CHULLS HU1 35 H4
Portland Pl CHULLN HU2 2 A2
Portland St CHULLN HU2 35 H2
Portmadoc Cl BRAN HU7 9 F3
Portobello St HULLE HU9 26 A4
Posterngate CHULLS HU1 2 D4
Potterill La BRAN HU7 15 F5
Poultney Garth HEDON HU12 41 F3
Premier Gv SUL/NEW HU5 * 23 G3
Prescott Av BR/NC/SC HU15 44 C4
Preston La BTNUH DN18 53 E4
Preston Rd HEDON HU12 40 D2
HULLE HU9 25 H5
SPR/BIL HU11 17 H5
Pretoria Av CHULLW HU3 * 34 D4
Pretoria St CHULLW HU3 34 D4
Pretoria Vls SUL/NEW HU5 * 23 G4
Priestgate BRAN HU7 15 F5
BTNUH DN18 53 E4
Primrose Dr SUL/NEW HU5 34 A1
Primrose Pk BEV HU17 7 H3
Primrose Vls HESSLE HU13 * 49 E1
Prince Charles Dr BTNUH DN18 53 F5
Prince Philip Dr BTNUH DN18 53 F5
Princes Av HEDON HU12 40 C3
HESSLE HU13 49 E3
SUL/NEW HU5 35 G1
Princes Dock St CHULLS HU1 2 C4
Princes Gdns BEV HU17 6 D1
Princes Quay CHULLS HU1 * 2 C4
Prince's Rd SUL/NEW HU5 23 G4
Princess Dr BTNUH DN18 53 F5
Princess Gdns BEV HU17 * 6 D1
SUL/NEW HU5 * 23 G4
Princess Gv CHULLW HU3 * 35 F3
Princess St CHULLN HU2 2 D1
Princess Wy BEV HU17 6 C4
Prince St CHULLS HU1 2 D4
Priory Av NF/SW HU14 46 D4
Priory Cl NF/SW HU14 31 F4
Priory Crs COT/SKID HU16 11 H5
Priory Dr SUL/NEW HU5 22 B4
Priory Farm Dr ANLPK/PPK HU4 50 B2
Priory Gv ANLPK/PPK HU4 34 B5
Priory La BRWUH DN19 55 E3
Priory Rd BEV HU17 7 F1
COT/SKID HU16 21 H1
SUL/NEW HU5 22 A3
Priory Wy ANLPK/PPK HU4 49 G3
Prospect Pl HULLE HU9 3 G2
Prospect St CHULLN HU2 2 A2
Providence Crs BTNUH DN18 52 D4
Providence Rw CHULLW HU3 36 A1
Prunus Av ANL/KKEL HU10 21 F5
Pryme St ANL/KKEL HU10 33 F3
CHULLN HU2 2 A2
Pulcroft Rd HESSLE HU13 48 D2
Pulman St CHULLW HU3 35 E2
Purton Gv BRAN HU7 14 C4
Putney Cl SINGS HU8 25 G1
Pykestone Cl BRAN HU7 9 G5
Pyruss Dr ANLPK/PPK HU4 49 H2

Q

The Quadrant HULLN HU6 22 D1
Quaker La BEV HU17 4 C5
Quantock Cl CHULLW HU3 35 H4
Quarrington Gv BRAN HU7 9 F5
Quay St CHULLS HU1 2 D3
Quebec Dr COT/SKID HU16 21 E1
Queen Elizabeth Wy BTNUH DN18 53 F5
Queen's Aly CHULLS HU1 2 E5
Queen's Av BTNUH DN18 53 E3
Queensbury Wy NF/SW HU14 31 E5
Queen's Cl COT/SKID HU16 11 H4
Queens Dock Av CHULLS HU1 2 C3
Queensdock Av CHULLS HU1 2 D3
Queen's Dock Av CHULLS HU1 2 D3
Queens Dr COT/SKID HU16 11 G4
Queens Gdns SUL/NEW HU5 * 23 F4
Queensgate BEV HU17 6 D2
Queen's Ga COT/SKID HU16 11 H4
Queen's Gate St CHULLW HU3 35 F4
Queensmead BEV HU17 6 C4
Queens Rd BEV HU17 5 F4
SUL/NEW HU5 23 G4
Queen St BTNUH DN18 53 E3
CHULLS HU1 2 D5
Queen's Wy COT/SKID HU16 11 H4
The Queensway HULLN HU6 13 F3
Queen Victoria Sq CHULLS HU1 * 2 C3
Quillcourt HULLN HU6 12 C4
Quilter Av ANLPK/PPK HU4 33 H4
Quilter Dr SPR/BIL HU11 17 F4
The Quorum ANLPK/PPK HU4 50 C1

R

Radcliffe Garth BR/NC/SC HU15 42 D3
Raglan Av SUL/NEW HU5 * 23 G3
Raglan St SUL/NEW HU5 23 G3
Raich Carter Wy HULLN HU6 13 F2
Railway St BEV HU17 5 E5
CHULLS HU1 2 C5
Rainham Cl SINGS HU8 15 G3
Rainhill Ct SUL/NEW HU5 23 E4
Rainhill Rd SUL/NEW HU5 23 E4
Rainswood Cl BRAN HU7 9 F5
Raleigh Dr HULLE HU9 37 F3
SPR/BIL HU11 19 E1
Ramblers La BTNUH DN18 52 C3
Ramsden Av BTNUH DN18 52 D4
Ramsden Ct BEV HU17 5 F5
Ramsden Pl COT/SKID HU16 21 F1
Ramsgate Cl SINGS HU8 15 G4
Rands Est HEDON HU12 29 E5
Randsfield Av BR/NC/SC HU15 44 B4
Rangely Cl BRAN HU7 9 G5
Rannoch Cl BRAN HU7 9 G4
Ransome Wy BR/NC/SC HU15 44 C3
Rauceby Cl BRAN HU7 9 F5
Ravendale BTNUH DN18 53 F5
Ravenspur Rd SPR/BIL HU11 17 G4
Raven St HULLE HU9 37 F2
Rawcliffe Gv ANLPK/PPK HU4 34 B5
Rawdale Cl BR/NC/SC HU15 42 D2
Rawling Wy CHULLW HU3 35 G4
Raywell Cl ANL/KKEL HU10 33 F2
Raywell St CHULLN HU2 2 B1
Raywood Vls CHULLW HU3 * 35 G4
Reading Room Yd NF/SW HU14 46 D4
Recreation Park La BEV HU17 4 D4
Rectory La HEDON HU12 28 D4
Redbourne St CHULLW HU3 35 F4
Redcar St SINGS HU8 36 C1
Redcliff Dr NF/SW HU14 46 D5
Redcliff Rd HESSLE HU13 48 D4
Redfern Cl CHULLW HU3 35 H4
Redhill Pk HULLN HU6 22 C1
Red House Farm HEDON HU12 40 B3
Redland Dr ANL/KKEL HU10 32 C1
Red Lion Ct ANL/KKEL HU10 * 33 E3
Redmire Cl BRAN HU7 9 G5
Redruth Cl BRAN HU7 15 E5
The Redwoods ANL/KKEL HU10 20 C4
Reeds La HULLE HU9 25 H4
Reed St CHULLN HU2 2 B2
Reform St CHULLN HU2 2 C1
Regency Ct BTNUH DN18 52 C3
Regent Cl ANL/KKEL HU10 21 E5
CHULLW HU3 35 G3
Regents Ct COT/SKID HU16 11 G5
Regent St BEV HU17 6 D1
Regina Crs SUL/NEW HU5 23 E4
Regis Ct HULLE HU9 26 B3
Register Sq BEV HU17 4 D5
Reigate Cl SINGS HU8 26 A2
Reldene Dr SUL/NEW HU5 33 H2
Renfrew St SUL/NEW HU5 35 F1
Rensburg St HULLE HU9 25 F5
Repton Dr BRAN HU7 25 F1
Reservoir Rd HULLN HU6 24 C2
Retford Gv HULLE HU9 27 E5
Revenser Ct HEDON HU12 41 F4
Reynolds Cl NF/SW HU14 45 H4
Reynoldson St SUL/NEW HU5 23 F4
Rhodes St CHULLW HU3 34 D4
Rhyl Cl BRAN HU7 9 F3
Ribble Av CHULLW HU3 * 35 F5
Ribblesdale BRAN HU7 14 C5
Ribble St CHULLW HU3 35 F5
Ribycourt HULLN HU6 12 C4
Riccall Cl HULLN HU6 13 E5
Richardson Rd HEDON HU12 40 C4
Richmond Gdns BEV HU17 6 C3
Richmond Rd HESSLE HU13 49 E2
Richmond St SUL/NEW HU5 23 F5
Richmond Wk BEV HU17 6 C3
Richmond Wy BEV HU17 6 C4
Ridgestone Av SPR/BIL HU11 17 E5
Ridgeway Rd SUL/NEW HU5 33 H2
Riding Fields Sq BEV HU17 5 F5
The Ridings BEV HU17 4 B3
COT/SKID HU16 11 F5
NF/SW HU14 46 D4
SUL/NEW HU5 33 G1
Ridsdale BRAN HU7 14 B4
Rievaulx Ct BRAN HU7 * 24 C2
Rigby Cl BEV HU17 4 C2
Rillington Av COT/SKID HU16 21 G1
Rimswell Gv HULLE HU9 26 A4
Ring Beck La BR/NC/SC HU15 43 E5
Ringrose St CHULLW HU3 34 D4
Ringstead Garth BRAN HU7 14 C1
Ripley Cl HULLN HU6 13 F4
Riplingham Rd ANL/KKEL HU10 20 A5
Ripon Av BEV HU17 6 D3
Ripon Wy HULLE HU9 37 E1
Risby Gv HULLN HU6 22 D1
Risby Pl BEV HU17 6 D2
The Rise NF/SW HU14 46 D3
Rise Wk CHULLW HU3 * 35 G4
Rishworth Cl BRAN HU7 9 G4
Riston St CHULLW HU3 35 G5
Rivelin Pk BRAN HU7 13 H1
Riverbank Ri BTNUH DN18 52 C3
River Gv ANLPK/PPK HU4 50 C1
Riversdale HULLE HU9 * 25 F5
Riversdale Rd HULLN HU6 13 G5
Riverside Ct HESSLE HU13 48 D5
River Vw BTNUH DN18 53 F5
Riverview Av NF/SW HU14 46 C5
Riverview Gdns BRAN HU7 14 A4
Riverview Rd BEV HU17
Rix Rd BRAN HU7 2
Robert Wood Av BEV HU17
Robin Cl BR/NC/SC HU15 4
Robinia Dr ANLPK/PPK HU4 5
Robinson Rw CHULLS HU1
Robinswood Dr BRAN HU7 1
Roborough Cl BRAN HU7 1
Robson Av HULLN HU6 1
Robson Wy BRAN HU7 1
HEDON HU12 4
SINGS HU8 1
Rochester Av ANLPK/PPK HU4 4
Rockford Av SINGS HU8 2
Rockford Gv SINGS HU8 2
Rodney Cl CHULLN HU2 3
Roger Garth ANL/KKEL HU10 2
Rokeby Av ANLPK/PPK HU4 3
Rokeby Cl ANLPK/PPK HU4 3
BEV HU17
Rokeby Pk ANLPK/PPK HU4 3
Roland Av CHULLW HU3 * 3
Rolston Cl HULLE HU9 2
Romford Gv HULLE HU9 2
Romney Gdns SUL/NEW HU5 2
Ronaldsway Cl HULLE HU9 2
Ronson Cl HULLE HU9 2
Rookley Cl SINGS HU8 2
Roos Cl BEV HU17
Roper St CHULLS HU1
Ropery Cl BEV HU17
Ropery La BTNUH DN18 5
Ropery St CHULLW HU3 3
Rosamond St CHULLW HU3 3
Rose Av CHULLW HU3 * 3
Rosebery Av SUL/NEW HU5 * 2
Rosebery St CHULLW HU3 3
Rosebury Vls HULLE HU9 * 3
Rosedale HULLE HU9 * 2
Rosedale Av HULLE HU9 2
Rosedale Gv SUL/NEW HU5 3
Rosedale Vls HULLE HU9 * 3
Rosedale Wk BEV HU17
Rosedene Vls SUL/NEW HU5 * 2
Rosemary Wy BEV HU17
Rosemount Cl HULLN HU6 1
Rosemount Gra HESSLE HU13 4
Rose Vls HULLE HU9 * 3
Rosewood Cl ANLPK/PPK HU4 3
Rosey Rw HULLE HU9
Roslyn Av SUL/NEW HU5 * 3
Roslyn Crs HEDON HU12 4
Roslyn Rd CHULLW HU3 3
Rosmead St HULLE HU9 3
Rosmead Vls HULLE HU9 * 3
Rothesay Av SUL/NEW HU5 * 2
Rothesay Cl HULLE HU9 2
Rotterdam Rd BRAN HU7 2
The Roundway ANLPK/PPK HU4 3
Routh Av BEV HU17
Rowan Av BEV HU17
Rowan Cl BRWUH DN19 5
Rowland Av HULLE HU9 *
Rowley Gv HULLN HU6 2
Rowlston Gv HULLE HU9 2
Roxburgh St SUL/NEW HU5 3
Roxton Hall Dr NF/SW HU14 4
Royale Ct HULLE HU9 2
Royal Garth BEV HU17
Royal Wk COT/SKID HU16 2
Royston Gv SINGS HU8 2
Rudston Gv HULLE HU9 2
Rufforth Garth BRAN HU7 1
Rugby St CHULLW HU3 3
Rugmere Cl CHULLW HU3 3
Ruislip Cl SINGS HU8 2
Runcorn Garth ANLPK/PPK HU4 4
Runnymede Wy BRAN HU7 1
Ruskin Av CHULLW HU3 * 3
Ruskin St CHULLW HU3 3
Ruskin Wy BR/NC/SC HU15 4
Russell St CHULLN HU2 3
Rustenburg St HULLE HU9 2
Ruston Wy BEV HU17
Ruswarp Gv HULLN HU6 1
Rutherglen Dr HULLE HU9 2
Rutland Rd SUL/NEW HU5 3
Rutland Ter BRAN HU7 * 1
Rydale Ct SUL/NEW HU5 2
The Rydales SUL/NEW HU5 2
Rydal Gv COT/SKID HU16 1
SUL/NEW HU5 * 2
Ryde Av SUL/NEW HU5 2
Ryde St SUL/NEW HU5 2
Rye Crs BR/NC/SC HU15 4
Ryedale BR/NC/SC HU15 4
Ryedale Gv HULLE HU9 3
Ryehill Gv HULLE HU9 2
Ryland Vls HULLE HU9 * 2

S

Sable Cl ANLPK/PPK HU4 5
Sabrina Ct SINGS HU8
Sackville Cl BEV HU17
Sacred Ga HEDON HU12 4
Saddleworth Cl BRAN HU7
Saffrondale ANL/KKEL HU10 3
Sage Cl BEV HU17
Sailors Whf HULLE HU9
Sainsbury Wy HESSLE HU13 4
St Abbs Cl HULLE HU9
St Aidan Wy HULLE HU9 2
St Albans Cl BEV HU17
St Ambrose Ct BRAN HU7 1
St Andrews Mt ANL/KKEL HU10 3
St Andrew St BEV HU17
St Andrews Vls SUL/NEW HU5 * 2
St Andrews Wy SINGS HU8 2
St Anne's Cl BEV HU17
St Anne's Dr COT/SKID HU16 1
St Anne's Wk BR/NC/SC HU15 4
St Annington Dr SINGS HU8
St Anthony's Dr HEDON HU12 4
St Anthony's Pk HEDON HU12 4

Acknowledgements

Schools address data provided by Education Direct.

Petrol station information supplied by Johnsons.

Garden centre information provided by:

Garden Centre Association ⬤ Britains best garden centres

Wyevale Garden Centres 🌷

The statement on the front cover of this atlas is sourced, selected and quoted from a reader comment and feedback form received in 2004

Street by Street QUESTIONNAIRE

Dear Atlas User
Your comments, opinions and recommendations are very important to us.
So please help us to improve our street atlases by taking a few minutes
to complete this simple questionnaire.

You do not need a stamp (unless posted outside the UK). If you do not want to remove
this page from your street atlas, then photocopy it or write your answers on a plain sheet
of paper.

Send to: Marketing Assistant, AA Publishing, 14th Floor Fanum House,
Freepost SCE 4598, Basingstoke RG21 4GY

ABOUT THE ATLAS...

Please state which city / town / county you bought:

_____

Where did you buy the atlas? (City, Town, County)

_____

For what purpose? (please tick all applicable)

To use in your local area ☐ **To use on business or at work** ☐

Visiting a strange place ☐ **In the car** ☐ **On foot** ☐

Other (please state)

_____

Have you ever used any street atlases other than AA Street by Street?

Yes ☐ No ☐

If so, which ones?

_____

Is there any aspect of our street atlases that could be improved?
(Please continue on a separate sheet if necessary)

_____
_____
_____
_____

ML152y

continued overleaf

Please list the features you found most useful:

_____

_____

Please list the features you found least useful:

_____

_____

_____

LOCAL KNOWLEDGE...

Local knowledge is invaluable. Whilst every attempt has been made to make the information contained in this atlas as accurate as possible, should you notice any inaccuracies, please detail them below (if necessary, use a blank piece of paper) or e-mail us at _streetbystreet@theAA.com_

_____

_____

_____

ABOUT YOU...

Name (Mr/Mrs/Ms) _____

Address _____

Postcode _____

Daytime tel no _____

E-mail address _____

Which age group are you in?

Under 25 ☐   **25-34** ☐   **35-44** ☐   **45-54** ☐   **55-64** ☐   **65+** ☐

Are you an AA member? **YES** ☐   **NO** ☐

Do you have Internet access? **YES** ☐   **NO** ☐

Thank you for taking the time to complete this questionnaire. Please send it to us as soon as possible, and remember, you do not need a stamp (unless posted outside the UK).

We may use information we hold about you to telephone or email you about other products and services offered by the AA, we do NOT disclose this information to third parties.

Please tick here if you do not wish to hear about products and services from the AA. ☐